D1326102

Cocktails & Rock Tales

Cocktails & Rock Tales

200 drinks to shake,
rattle & roll with

Jane Rocca

Hardie Grant Books

Published in 2008 by
Hardie Grant Books
85 High Street
Prahran, Victoria 3181, Australia
www.hardiegrant.com.au

Text © Jane Rocca 2008
Illustrations © Trisha Garner and Michelle Mackintosh 2008
All photography © **Tim James** except: Photographs by **iStockphoto** on p. 36 (cassette tape), p. 91 (records, tape and headphones), p. 92 (microphone), pp. 96/7 (records), pp. 132/3 (Shiva) and pp. 160/1 (record). Photographs by **Trisha Garner** on p.vi–ix (brick wall), p. X–1 (graffiti on pavement), p. 6 (badge), p. 10 (badge), p. 18 (skull), p. 21 (after the gig), p. 42 (yellow plastic), p. 46 (beads and lollipops), p. 55 ("I Love Pop" doll), p. 98 (vespa box), p. 126 (badge) and p. 127 (patterned background). Photographs by **Michelle Mackintosh** on p. 4 (ripped paper), p. 10 (tag necklace), p. 13 (wing), p. 22 (wall background), p. 24 (ripped paper and wall background), p. 31 (leather bracelet and fishnet), p. 38 (ticket and pins), p. 39 (braces, badge and collar), pp. 40/1 (belt and wall background), p. 42 ("POP" letters) p. 44 (ripped paper), p. 45 (rainbow clip), p. 59, p. 60 (badge), p. 64 (ripped paper), p. 81 (ripped paper), p. 84 (ripped paper), p. 87 (flower clips), p. 102 (ripped paper and headphones), p. 105 (locket), p. 106 (heart), p. 109 (tickets), p. 111 (swan clasp), p.116 (badges), pp. 118/9, p.122 (ripped paper), p.140 (ripped paper), p. 142 (hairclips) p. 158 (ripped paper), p. 176 (ripped paper), p. 179 (record), pp. 184/5 (records) and p. 192 (records). Photographs by **Shutterstock** on p. 46 (yellow radio), p. 48 (cassette tape), pp. 54/55 (maracas and guitar), p. 67 (glasses), p. 81 (skateboard), p. 82 (wooden lettering), p. 85 (sunglasses), p. 88 (false eyelashes), p. 93 (bowtie) p. 94 (turntable), pp. 114/5 (heels), p. 123 (lava lamp), p. 124 (jack leads), p. 127 (guitar), p. 128 (effects pedal), p. 129 (drum), p. 131 (switches), p. 149 (red car), p. 150 (sunglasses), p. 154, p. 155 (radio), p. 161 (belt), p. 162, p. 165 (guitar case), p. 168 (harmonica), pp. 168/9 (banjo) and p. 190 (lights).

Cataloguing-in-Publication data is available from the National Library of Australia.
ISBN 9781740666497

Design by Trisha Garner and Michelle Mackintosh
Set in Serifa
Printed and bound in China by Toppan Leefung Printing Limited.

10 9 8 7 6 5 4 3

Contents

GLASS TYPES

COLADA GLASS

OLD-FASHIONED GLASS

TIKI MUG

HURRICANE GLASS

BOSTON GLASS
& SHAKER

GOBLET

HIGHBALL GLASS

SHOT GLASS

COUPETTE GLASS

GLASS TYPES

BEER MUG

MARTINI GLASS

PINT GLASS

WINE GLASS

PILSNER GLASS

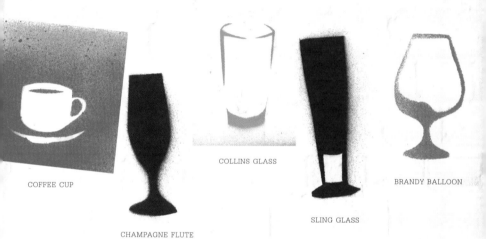

COFFEE CUP

CHAMPAGNE FLUTE

COLLINS GLASS

SLING GLASS

BRANDY BALLOON

SYRUPS AND INFUSIONS

[x] SYRUPS

Sugar syrup – also known as simple syrup or bar syrup, is used in many cocktails to offset the tartness or strong alcohol flavour of some drinks. Syrups are used instead of plain sugar, as they are easily mixed with other liquids. To make a simple sugar syrup stir two parts sugar into one part hot water in a saucepan. Heat gently until the sugar dissolves then bring to the boil. Remove from the heat and leave to cool before using.

Flavoured syrups – are made by infusing a simple sugar syrup with fruits, spices or herbs. Anything from vanilla pods, coffee beans or rose petals may be used.

Gomme syrup – this is a sugar syrup made with the highest ratio of sugar to water possible. Gum arabic is added which acts as an emulsifier, prevents the sugar from crystallizing and adds a lovely smooth texture. To make gomme syrup, bring sugar and water to the boil then add gum arabic powder dissolved in water. Strain for use.

INFUSING SPIRITS

[1]

Many spirits now come in different flavours, but sometimes you will want to make your own homemade infusions.

You can add flavour to alcohol in two ways:

Infusion/maceration:
Place the ingredients with the alcohol in an air-tight container until the flavour is absorbed to your liking (a few days). Store the container at room temperature, out of direct sulight. You will need to check the infusion every day as after a week the alcohol can take on a stale or bitter flavour, depending on the ingredient.

Pan infusion:
Heat the alcohol in a saucepan with the ingredients until it simmers. Let it sit for up to three hours, then strain alcohol into its original bottle. This method is only suitable for fruit- and sugar-based infusions – not flowers.

LET THERE BE ROCK

Rock 'n' roll changes your life and complicates it long after you lose your virginity to the sounds of an anthem you'll never forget. Its riffs knock on your door louder than a neighbour's request to turn them down. Rock demands that you stay out all night drinking 'till you can no longer stand. And while it pronounces you almighty, it's a constant reminder of a time when you rocked harder than perhaps you do now.

With Rock music there's no tomorrow – it's all about the here and now. It offers itself up to those who want more than ordinary and encourages those who seek adventure to take risks and live life to the fullest.

The decadent nature of Rock 'n' roll means there are no excuses for those who can't keep up. And not everyone can survive its antics, even if, like AC/DC's Bon Scott, they were once at the very helm of the genre. Some rock heroes, like Keith Richards from the Stones hang in there by the skin of their teeth, while others, such as Motörhead's Lemmy, slow down for no-one. But in the end rock is just as much about the myth as it is about the icons who live and breathe it.

There's the backstage romancing, the tour-bus trekking, the post-gig drink-ups… but heck, that's what it's all about: collecting as many debauched stories as possible in the space of a wild night out. Because only Rock can cradle you in its evil arms and spit you out in the morning, leaving you begging for one more serve.

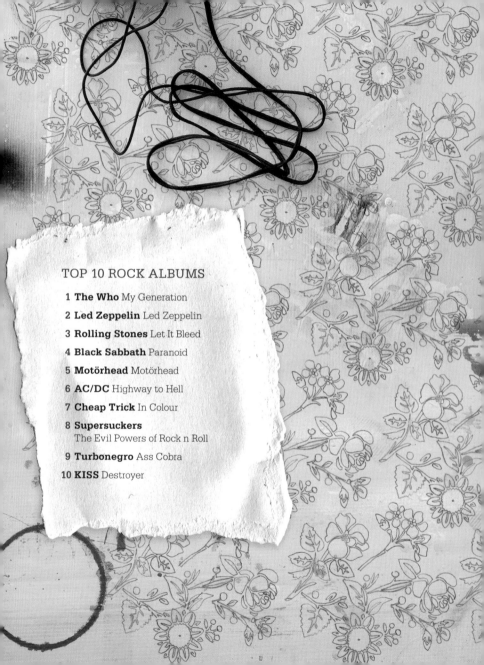

TOP 10 ROCK ALBUMS

1 **The Who** My Generation

2 **Led Zeppelin** Led Zeppelin

3 **Rolling Stones** Let It Bleed

4 **Black Sabbath** Paranoid

5 **Motörhead** Motörhead

6 **AC/DC** Highway to Hell

7 **Cheap Trick** In Colour

8 **Supersuckers**
The Evil Powers of Rock n Roll

9 **Turbonegro** Ass Cobra

10 **KISS** Destroyer

LIQUID SPEEDBALL
Highball glass

60 ml bourbon
splash of cola
lemon wedges to garnish

Pour bourbon into highball glass over
ice and top up with cola. Throw in some
lemon wedges to garnish.

ROCKAWAY BEACH
Highball glass

[5]

30 ml blackcurrant-infused vodka
30 ml lychee liqueur
splash of sparkling pink
  grapefruit juice
3 lime wedges
fresh lychee to garnish

Build liquids in highball glass on ice.
Squeeze in lime wedges then discard
them. Garnish with lychee.

SMELL OF FEMALE
Pilsner glass

5 mint sprigs, roughly torn
4 watermelon chunks
30 ml vodka
15 ml watermelon liqueur
15 ml rosewater
splash of soda water
extra mint sprig to garnish

Muddle mint leaves and watermelon in shaker. Add all remaining ingredients except for garnish and shake with ice. Pour into pilsner glass and top up with soda water. Garnish with a mint sprig.

THIN LIZZIE
Champagne flute

15 ml crème de fraise
15 ml tequila liqueur
splash of Champagne
strawberry to garnish

Pour crème de fraise and tequila into flute and top with Champagne. Garnish with a strawberry.

BEASTS OF BOURBON
Old-fashioned glass

45 ml bourbon
15 ml vanilla syrup
¼ teaspoon ginger
45 ml peach purée
45 ml sweet and sour mix
strip burnt orange peel to garnish

Shake all ingredients except for garnish
and pour into an old-fashioned glass.
Garnish with burnt orange peel.

WHOLE LOTTA LOVE
Sling glass

30 ml Pimms No.1 Cup
15 ml Cointreau
15 ml grapefruit-infused vodka
1 ½ tablespoons orange-cucumber salsa
60 ml apple juice
30 ml soda water
mint sprig to garnish

Build all ingredients except for garnish
over ice in sling glass. Garnish with mint
sprig and stir well before serving.

BLOODY BULL
Pint glass

celery salt
60 ml vodka
60 ml beef broth or bouillon
180 ml tomato juice
1 teaspoon of horseradish cream
1 teaspoon of Worcestershire sauce
dash of Tabasco
cracked black pepper

Moisten the rim of the glass and dip into
celery salt. Add ice cubes to glass and
stir in vodka, beef broth and tomato juice.
Stir in horseradish cream, Worcestershire
sauce and Tabasco and sprinkle with
black pepper.

COCK SUCKIN' COWBOY
Shot glass

butterscotch schnapps
Irish cream

Pour schnapps into shot glass.
Carefully layer the Irish cream by pouring
over the back of the spoon.

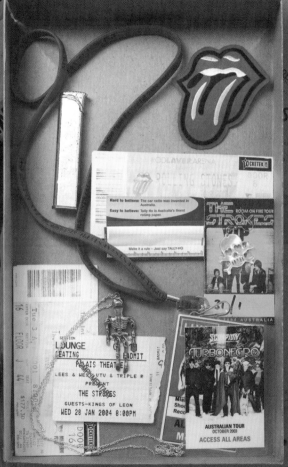

[10]

ABSINTHE DRIP
Martini glass

60 ml absinthe
1 sugar cube
splash of soda water

Pour absinthe into mixing glass over ice. Place sugar cube on top and slowly drip on soda water, until sugar dissolves. Mix well and strain into chilled martini glass.

CHERRY HOOKER
Highball glass

60 ml cherry brandy
splash of orange juice
lemon wedge to serve

Pour cherry brandy into highball glass over ice. Top up with orange juice and garnish with lemon wedge.

[11]

[12]

LAVA LAMP MARTINI
Martini glass

30 ml raspberry liqueur
30 ml honey
60 ml vodka

Mix the honey and raspberry liqueur
in a shot glass then pour into shaker
with vodka. Shake and strain into
martini glss.

THE PURPLE HAZE

Old-fashioned glass

45 ml vodka
15 ml black raspberry liqueur
splash of cranberry juice

Shake vodka and black raspberry liqueur with ice. Strain into an old-fashioned glass over ice and top up with cranberry juice.

BETWEEN THE SHEETS

[13]

Old-fashioned glass

30 ml white rum
15 ml cognac
90 ml passionfruit juice
15 ml lime juice
maraschino cherry to garnish

Combine all ingredients except for lime juice and garnish. Stir with ice then pour into old-fashioned glass. Top up with lime juice and garnish with cherry.

SCOTCH BERRY FARM
Martini glass

30 ml whisky
15 ml black raspberry liqueur
15 ml lime juice
60 ml cranberry juice

Shake all ingredients and pour into martini glass.

BATTERING RAM
Highball glass

45 ml silver rum
15 ml white rum
15 ml bourbon
60 ml orange juice
15 ml lemon juice
slice of orange to garnish

Shake all ingredients except for garnish and pour into highball glass. Garnish with orange slice

BLACK MAGIC

Old-fashioned glass

20 ml dark crème de cacao
20 ml chestnut liqueur
10 ml blackberry liqueur
20 ml blueberry purée
splash of lemon juice
chocolate shard to garnish

Combine all ingredients except for garnish in a mixing glass and stir. Pour into old-fashioned glass and garnish with a chocolate shard.

OTTO'S ORGASM

Shot glass

30 ml dark rum
15 ml Irish cream
15 ml ginger liqueur
candied ginger to garnish (optional)

Combine all ingredients except for
garnish and shake with ice. Strain
into shot glass and garnish with
candied ginger, if using.

TIKI-QUILA

Shot glass

30 ml tequila
15 ml triple sec
15 ml strawberry schnapps
15 ml pineapple juice
15 ml sour mix (lemon/lime juice)
slice of orange to garnish (optional)

Combine all ingredients except for garnish
and shake with ice. Strain into shot glass
and garnish with slice of orange, if using.

SHRUNKEN HEAD
Highball glass

45 ml dark rum
15 ml coconut rum
30 ml orange juice
splash of lemonade
slice of orange and maraschino
cherry to garnish

Pour both rums and orange juice
into ice-filled glass and top up with
lemonade. Garnish with slice of
orange and cherry.

OTTO'S OCTANE
Beer mug

30 ml pineapple rum
15 ml Kahlúa
15 ml banana liqueur
15 ml pineapple juice
big splash of rum
60 ml soda water
60 ml orange juice
slice of pineapple and maraschino
cherry to garnish

Fill beer mug with ice. Combine all
ingredients except for garnish in shaker.
Shake twice then pour into mug. Garnish
with pineapple and cherry.

SOUR TO THE 10TH POWER [19]
Martini glass

60 ml gin
30 ml lemon juice
15 ml chamomile syrup
30 ml ruby red grapefruit juice
thin slice of grapefruit to garnish

Shake all ingredients except for garnish
and double-strain into chilled martini
glass. Garnish with grapefruit slice on
rim of glass.

HEART OF STONE
Martini glass

3 dried apricots
45 ml Irish whiskey
15 ml Cointreau
20 ml lemon juice
15 ml elderflower cordial
15 ml red wine (preferably merlot)
3 extra dried apricots to garnish

Muddle dried apricots with whiskey and Cointreau in shaker. Add all remaining ingredients except for garnish and shake. Double-strain into chilled martini glass. Garnish with three dried apricots on a skewer placed across the top of the glass.

LITTLE RED ROOSTER
Martini glass

60 ml rye whiskey
10 ml peach liqueur
3 dashes of orange bitters
5 ml grenadine syrup
maraschino cherry to garnish

Shake all ingredients except for garnish and strain into martini glass. Garnish with maraschino cherry

Punk

RAW POWER

Punk is gritty, dirty, mean and possessed. Few musical genres shoot from the hip like punk does, or with such intense ammunition. Think of the raw power of Iggy Pop and The Stooges, with their thirst for stinky riffs and charged lyrics. Or The Clash and their political anthems, where heated discussion was embraced.

Punk might have been spawned in the 1970s, but it continues to leave an indelible mark on the music of subsequent generations. Take LA's influential punk band X as example. Here was a band charged on punk's high energy and melodic core; their single *Your Phone's Off The Hook* nailed Punk's slippery appeal.

From the New York Doll's Personality Crisis to the enigma that was the Dwarves, punk is about short, sharp bursts of anger, humour and unashamed pretensions. And then there was the Washington DC band, Minor Threat, whose song about youthful nostalgia, *Salad Days* rammed its message down our throats in a machine-gun manner. Punk is about as rebellious as it gets.

Punk's anti-establishment message is straightforward. It has inspired revolutions and made many want to pick up a guitar and protest. Mess with it if you dare, but Punk gets under your skin and inks its message into your DNA in a way that no other relationship could ever compete with.

TOP 10 PUNK RECORDS

1 **The Clash** The Clash

2 **X** Los Angeles

3 **The Real Kids** The Real Kids

4 **Black Flag** Damaged

5 **Dwarves** Blood Guts & Pussy

6 **New York Dolls** New York Dolls

7 **The Ramones** Rocket to Russia

8 **Sex Pistols** Never Mind the Bollocks

9 **The Stooges** Fun House

10 **Minor Threat** Out of Step

MINDSNARE
Martini glass

10 ml absinthe
45 ml 12 year old whisky
20 ml Grand Marnier
5 ml sweet Scotch liqueur

Fill martini glass with ice and stir in absinthe. Top up with water and set aside. Shake remaining ingredients with ice. Discard ice, absinthe and water and strain drink into the coated glass.

5,6,7,8

[25]

Collins glass

6 chunks of lime
5 dashes of bitters
60 ml rum
lime wedge to garnish

Muddle lime and bitters in shaker. Add rum and shake with ice. Strain into collins glass over crushed ice. Garnish with lime wedge.

UP YA GINGER
Sling glass

10 lime wedges
1 teaspoon finely chopped fresh ginger
45 ml honey-infused vodka
10 ml crème de gingembre
splash of ginger beer

Muddle lime and ginger in shaker. Add vodka and crème de gingembre and shake hard with ice. Dump into sling glass and top up with ginger beer.

INNER CITY DRAGON
Highball glass

¼ lime
sprig of fresh coriander
piece of fresh ginger
45 ml chilli-infused vodka
15 ml green ginger wine
splash of cranberry juice
splash of ginger beer
chilli and coriander leaves to garnish

Muddle lime, coriander and ginger in shaker. Add vodka and ginger wine and stir well with ice. Pour into highball glass and top up with cranberry juice and a splash of ginger beer. Garnish with chilli and coriander leaves.

AMARETTO SOUR
Old-fashioned glass

60 ml amaretto
30 ml lemon juice
1 tablespoon sugar, or to taste
1 small egg white
maraschino cherry to garnish

Combine amaretto, lemon juice and sugar in shaker with ice. Add egg white and shake hard for 30 seconds. Pour into a sugar-rimmed old-fashioned glass. Garnish with a maraschino cherry.

GORILLA SNOT
Large martini glass

30 ml crème de menthe
30 ml Irish cream

Blend crème de menthe with a big handful of ice (enough to ensure a good thick consistency). Spoon mixture into large martini glass. Pour on the Irish cream and serve with 2 short straws.

BREAKFAST MARGARITA

Martini glass

45 ml tequila
15 ml tequila liqueur
5 ml agave syrup
30 ml lemon juice
1 teaspoon marmalade
½ egg white
4 drops orange bitters
fat strip of lemon zest to garnish

Combine all ingredients, except bitters and garnish, in shaker. Shake and double-strain into martini glass. Splash bitters on top and garnish with rolled lemon zest.

THE PAPILLON

Martini glass

2 small cucumber wheels
45 ml gin
15 ml apple liqueur
20 ml lime juice
5 ml elderflower cordial
slice of cucumber to garnish

Muddle cucumber in shaker. Add all remaining ingredients except for garnish and shake with ice. Double-strain into martini glass and garnish with slice of cucumber.

HEP-CAT'S SAZERAC
Old-fashioned glass

10 ml whisky
40 ml rum
20 ml Tuaca
dash of orange bitters
orange zest to garnish

Fill old-fashioned glass with ice and stir in whisky. Top up with water and set aside. Stir remaining ingredients together in a mixing glass. Discard ice, whisky and water and pour drink into the coated glass. Garnish with orange zest.

JAMMIN' WITH THE BAND
Martini glass

2 teaspoons blood orange jam
40 ml gin
20 ml Campari
dash of orange bitters
15 ml lemon juice
10 ml pomegranate syrup

Shake ingredients and double-strain into martini glass.

BORDELLO

Old-fashioned glass

45 ml tequila
15 ml amaretto
30 ml pineapple juice

Shake all ingredients with ice.
Strain into old-fashioned glass.

LUX INTERIOR
Sling glass

3 lychees
¹/₃ teaspoon grated fresh ginger
1 teaspoon palm sugar
30 ml ginger-infused vodka
15 ml lychee liqueur
splash of ginger beer
extra lychee to garnish

Muddle lychees, ginger and sugar in shaker. Add vodka and liqueur and shake well with ice. Pour into sling glass. Top up with ginger beer and garnish with lychee.

ZOMBIE GHOST TRAIN
Martini glass

30 ml crème de menthe
15 ml white crème de cacao
15 ml Frangelico
15 ml cream
chocolate mint stick to garnish

Shake all ingredients except for garnish with ice and strain into chilled martini glass. Garnish with chocolate mint stick.

CORPSE GRINDER
Old-fashioned glass

½ kiwi fruit, quartered
½ lime, chopped
3 strawberries, halved
1 teaspoon brown sugar
45 ml kiwi-infused vodka
15 ml strawberry liqueur
extra kiwi fruit to garnish

Muddle kiwi fruit, lime and strawberries with sugar in shaker. Add vodka and strawberry liqueur and shake briefly with crushed ice. Serve in old-fashioned glass and top with more crushed ice. Garnish with kiwi fruit.

HAIRY DOG
Coffee cup with handle

45 ml cognac
15 ml Kahlúa
10 ml caramel syrup
vanilla ice-cream
30 ml fresh espresso
chocolate powder to dust

Combine cognac, Kahlúa and syrup in saucepan and heat gently. Press 1 cm vanilla ice-cream into bottom of coffee cup. Pour in hot mixture and top with fresh espresso to create crema. Serve coffee cup on a plate with spoon and chocolate dusting.

PIRATE BLAZER
Brandy balloon

60 ml rum
60 ml boiling water
10 ml cocoa syrup
10 ml honey water
1 teaspoon cinnamon powder
twist of orange to garnish

Heat two coffee steamers. Combine all ingredients except for garnish in jug and steam carefully. Toss into second hot coffee steamer then pour carefully into brandy balloon. Garnish with orange twist.

PEPE FIZZ
Highball glass

30 ml sloe gin
15 ml gin
10 ml walnut liqueur
25 ml lemon juice
dash of lemon bitters
dash of egg white
twist of lemon and walnut pieces
     to garnish

Combine all ingredients except for
garnish and shake with ice. Strain into
highball glass over ice. Garnish with
lemon twist and walnuts.

SHRUNKEN SKIRT
Highball glass

60 ml mango-infused rum
30 ml cranberry juice
30 ml lemonade or
**   lemon-lime soda**
splash of pineapple juice
slice of orange and maraschino
**   cherry to garnish**

Combine all ingredients except for
pineapple juice and shake twice.
Pour into highball glass over ice.
Top up with pineapple juice and
garnish with orange and cherry.

GIBSON

[37]

Martini glass

5–10 ml dry vermouth
30 ml gin
30 ml vodka
2 pearl onions to garnish

Fill mixing glass with ice and stir in
vermouth. Discard excess vermouth
depending on preferred level of dryness.
Stir again and strain into martini
glass. Garnish with 2 pearl onions on a
toothpick.

ALTERNATE CURRANT

Highball glass

40 ml gin
20 ml crème de mûres
15 ml elderflower syrup
30 ml lemon juice
1 teaspoon quince paste
splash of sparkling wine
twist of lemon to garnish

Shake all ingredients except for sparkling wine and garnish. Strain into highball glass over ice and top up with sparkling wine. Garnish with twist of lemon.

SLOE GIN SOUR

Coupette glass

45 ml sloe gin liqueur
15 ml Cointreau
10 ml gomme syrup
1 egg white
45 ml lemon juice
½ slice of lime to garnish (optional)

Combine all ingredients except for garnish in shaker. Add chunks of ice and shake very vigorously for at least 30 seconds to fluff up the egg white. Strain into a coupette glass and float lime slice, if using.

OLD TOM
Martini glass

5 cm piece cucumber, roughly chopped
60 ml gin
30 ml pink grapefruit juice
15 ml elderflower cordial
15 ml lemon juice
15 ml pear nectar
4 slices of cucumber to garnish

Muddle cucumber in shaker.
Add all remaining ingredients except
for garnish and shake with ice. Strain
into martini glass and garnish with slices
of cucumber.

SMOKE IN THE GRASS
Martini glass

splash smoky Scotch whisky
2 cm piece lemongrass
45 ml pomaranzca vodka
15 ml Cointreau
1 teaspoon orange and ginger
marmalade
dash of lime juice
30 ml apple juice
dash of bitters
thin sliver of fresh ginger to garnish

Rinse chilled cocktail glass with
whisky to coat.

Muddle the lemongrass in shaker.
Add all remaining ingredients except
for garnish and shake. Double-strain
into martini glass and garnish with
ginger sliver.

VANILLA MANHATTAN
Martini glass

15 ml Licor 43
15 ml vermouth rosso
45 ml Canadian whisky
orange zest and maraschino cherry
to garnish

Combine all ingredients except for
garnish in mixing glass with ice.
Stir then strain into martini glass.
Garnish with orange zest and
maraschino cherry.

NAUGHTY NELL

Beer mug

60 ml blueberry-infused vodka
15 ml grape liqueur
30 ml orange juice
30 ml lemonade
splash of soda water
twist of lemon to garnish

Combine all ingredients except for garnish in shaker. Shake twice then strain into beer mug. Garnish with twist of lemon.

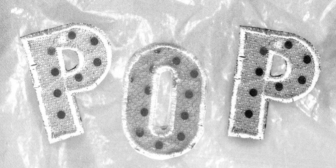

THESE BOOTS ARE MADE FOR WALKING

Good pop songs are not just chart-toppers, they are contagious ditties with a chorus you can't ignore and a beat that brings you to your feet. They can trigger memories from your past that only finding an old diary can truly unlock. They leave you aching for more and repeat in your mind long after you hear the song played.

The Beach Boys got it absolutely right with *Wouldn't It Be Nice* – a gentle blend of complex harmonies and tender lyrics that wash over you like a warm soapy bath. The band perfectly captured a youthful essence of American culture, and when you listen to their music some thirty years after it was penned, it still feels like it was written just for you.

Pop is sentimental; it's playful and danceable. Songs that inspire you to get up and move, like Madonna's *Holiday* or Outkast's *Hey Ya!*, hint that when the beat is right, the catchy wordplay will follow.

The Beatles gave birth to pop with songs such as *Can't Buy Me Love*. Cheap Trick hooked us with *I Want You to Want Me* and the Undertones brought mod and pop to the dance floor with *Teenage Kicks*. A decade later The Verve found pop bliss in the druggy mysticism of *The Drugs Don't Work*, The truth is that Pop is like a candy addiction – it's deliciously good and has you lusting after a second scoopful.

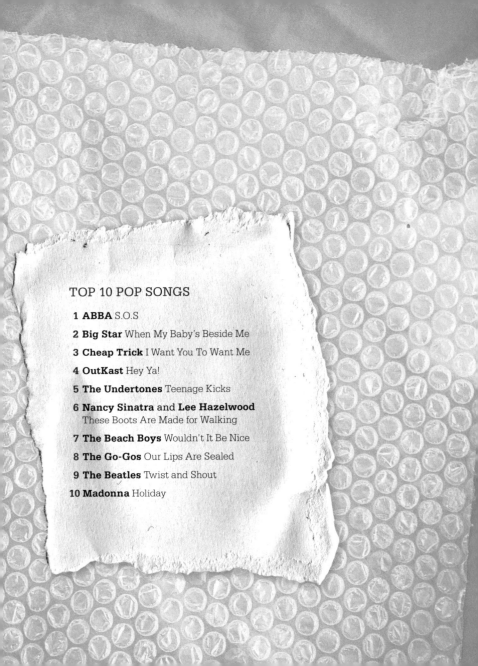

TOP 10 POP SONGS

1 **ABBA** S.O.S

2 **Big Star** When My Baby's Beside Me

3 **Cheap Trick** I Want You To Want Me

4 **OutKast** Hey Ya!

5 **The Undertones** Teenage Kicks

6 **Nancy Sinatra** and **Lee Hazelwood**
These Boots Are Made for Walking

7 **The Beach Boys** Wouldn't It Be Nice

8 **The Go-Gos** Our Lips Are Sealed

9 **The Beatles** Twist and Shout

10 **Madonna** Holiday

SPRING MARTINI
Martini glass

30 ml gin
15 ml tawny port
15 ml crème de mûres
30 ml cranberry juice
15 ml lemon juice
5 ml balsamic vinegar reduction
dash of egg white
5–6 raspberries on skewer to garnish

Shake all ingredients except for garnish
and double-strain into martini glass.
Garnish with skewered raspberries.

JULIA GRACE
Sling glass

5 cm peeled cucumber,
   roughly chopped
½ green apple, peeled and chopped
5 ml gomme syrup
pinch of salt
30 ml gin
30 ml vodka
30 ml clear apple juice
splash of dry ginger ale

Muddle cucumber, apple, gomme
and salt in shaker. Add ice and shake
vigorously. Pour into sling glass and top
up with dry ginger ale.

CHUCK BERRY
Martini glass

4 raspberries
2 strawberries
30 ml raspberry-infused vodka
15 ml black raspberry liqueur
15 ml crème de cacao
**strawberry and chocolate flakes
    to garnish**

Blend all ingredients except for
garnish with ice. Pour into martini
glass and garnish with a strawberry
and chocolate flakes.

LITTLE RED CORVETTE
Coupette glass

45 ml vodka
30 ml passionfruit liqueur
splash of Cointreau
60 ml cranberry juice
lemon wheel to garnish

Shake all ingredients except for garnish
and pour into glass over ice. Garnish
with lemon wheel.

PLATINUM BLOND

Martini glass

60 ml vodka
30 ml coconut rum
60 ml pineapple juice
maraschino cherry to garnish

Shake all ingredients except for
garnish and strain into martini glass.
Garnish with cherry.

BEACH BUM

Highball glass

30 ml vodka
30 ml coconut rum
30 ml crème de bananes
45 ml pineapple juice
45 ml grapefruit juice
banana slice to garnish

Shake all ingredients except for
garnish and pour into glass over ice.
Garnish with banana.

POP THESE BOOTS ARE MADE FOR WALKING

MIDNIGHT OIL
Old-fashioned glass

20 ml rye whiskey
20 ml cognac
10 ml vermouth rosso
5 dashes of bitters

Shake all ingredients and strain into old-fashioned glass over ice.

BOTANICAL
Highball glass

30 ml blackcurrant-infused vodka
20 ml Aperol
5 ml peach schnapps
5 ml apple schnapps
60 ml cranberry juice
juice of ¼ fresh lime
30 ml orange juice
twist of grapefruit to garnish

Combine all ingredients except orange juice and garnish and shake with ice. Pour into highball. Float orange juice and garnish with twist of grapefruit.

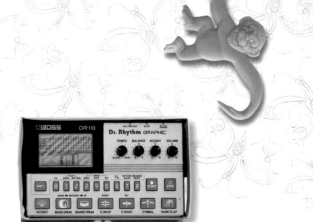

RUM CHA
Boston glass

45 ml rum
20 ml port
15 ml vanilla liqueur
1 teaspoon butter
6 rum-soaked raisins
15 ml 5-spice-infused sugar syrup
3 cloves
grated nutmeg
grated cinnamon stick

In a mixing glass combine rum, port
and vanilla liquor. Stir in butter, raisins,
5-spice syrup, cloves, nutmeg and
cinnamon. Pour mixture into teapot
and add hot water. Stir then pour into
boston glass.

LEMON MERINGUE PIE
Martini glass

30 ml citrus-infused vodka
30 ml vanilla-infused vodka
15 ml limoncello
2 teaspoons lemon curd
30 ml cream
5 ml cinnamon-infused sugar syrup
baby meringue to garnish

Combine all ingredients except for
garnish in shaker and stir to dissolve
lemon curd. Add ice and shake. Double-
strain into martini glass and float baby
meringue to garnish.

GRAPE WALL OF CHINA
Martini glass

4 grapes
30 ml Pisco Blanco
    (South American brandy)
15 ml apple liqueur
30 ml lemon juice
extra grape to garnish

Muddle grapes in shaker then add
liquids. Shake and double-strain strain
into martini glass and garnish with grape
on rim of glass.

CONFEDERATES JULEP
Highball glass

50 ml bourbon
10 ml white crème de cacao
3 dashes of peach bitters
1 teaspoon sugar syrup
8–10 fresh mint leaves
20 ml peach tea soda
mint sprig to garnish

Combine bourbon, crème de cacao
and bitters in highball glass with syrup
and 4 of the mint leaves. Press lightly to
bruise mint. Half-fill glass with crushed
ice and stir. Add 4 more mint leaves and
ice and top up with soda. Garnish with
mint sprig.

FOOL'S GOLD SMASH
Goblet

50 ml tequila
10 ml apricot liqueur
2 heaped teaspoons apricot jam
2 drops of rosewater
10 ml lemon juice
1 dash of bitters
lemon twist to garnish

Shake all ingredients except for garnish and double-strain into wine goblet. Garnish with lemon twist.

PLANTATION CAIPIRINHA
Old-fashioned glass

¾ lime, cut into chunks
1 teaspoon brown sugar
15 ml vanilla syrup
15 ml port
50 ml Sagatiba Pura Cachaca
   (Brazilian rum)

Muddle lime and sugar with syrup and port. Build Cachaca and crushed ice in a glass. Top with more crushed ice.

SWEATSHOP SWIZZLE
Highball glass

45 ml rum
30 ml pomegranate juice
15 ml grapefruit juice
15 ml falernum syrup
1 dash of bitters
1 dash of orange bitters
julienne lime and grapefruit peel
    on skewer to garnish

Combine all ingredients except for garnish in highball glass. Fill three-quarters full with crushed ice and swizzle till cold. Top with more crushed ice and garnish with lime and grapefruit skewer.

DOUBLE DRAGON: YIN
Martini glass

dash of squid ink
45 ml tequila
15 ml coffee liqueur
15 ml walnut syrup
3 dashes of bitters
white chocolate button to garnish

Combine all ingredients except for garnish in shaker. Shake and double-strain into a martini glass and garnish with a white chocolate button.

DOUBLE DRAGON: YANG [55]
Martini glass

30 ml rum
15 ml yellow Chartreuse
15 ml white chocolate syrup
30 ml half and half (cream and milk)
dark chocolate button to garnish

Shake all ingredients except for garnish
and double-strain into martini glass.
Garnish with a dark chocolate button.

SIXTEEN DOLLAR SAKE
Martini glass

45 ml sake
20 ml sloe gin
15 ml lavender-infused sugar syrup
30 ml lemon juice
3 dried cranberries to garnish

Combine all ingredients except for
garnish in shaker. Shake and strain
into a martini glass. Garnish with dried
cranberries on a skewer.

MATERIAL GIRL
Martini glass

3 strawberries
2 lime wedges
30 ml vanilla-infused vodka
20 ml Frangelico
10 ml black raspberry liqueur
30 ml pear juice
mixed berries to garnish

Muddle strawberries in shaker, then add
lime and muddle again. Add liquids and
shake well with ice. Double-strain into
a chilled martini glass. Garnish with
mixed berries on a skewer.

EVITA
Martini glass

45 ml Scotch whisky
15 ml Licor 43
15 ml sauvignon blanc
30 ml cloudy apple juice
5 ml vanilla syrup
dash of lemon juice
apple ring and lemon zest to garnish

Shake all ingredients except for garnish
with ice. Double-strain into a chilled
martini glass. Float apple ring and top
with lemon zest to garnish.

DIAMOND GLOVE
Highball glass

60 ml Irish whiskey
15 ml sour apple liqueur
15 ml apple juice
10 ml cinnamon syrup
3–5 mint leaves
45 ml ginger beer
apple slices to garnish

Combine whiskey, liqueur, juice and syrup in a shaker. Shake with ice and pour into highball glass. Slap the mint in your hands and stir into drink. Top up with ginger beer and ice if needed. Garnish with fanned apple slices.

POP TART
Martini glass

45 ml vodka
30 ml cloudy apple juice
5 ml bitters

Shake all ingredients with a good scoop of ice. Strain into sugar-rimmed martini glass.

POP HER CHERRY
Martini glass

30 ml vodka
15 ml cherry liqueur
5 ml maraschino cherry juice
10 ml crème de cacao
maraschino cherry to garnish

Shake all ingredients except for garnish
with a good scoop of ice. Double-strain
into chilled martini glass and garnish
with cherry.

HOT 100
Old-fashioned glass

30 ml whisky liqueur
15 ml green ginger wine
15 ml lemon juice
20 ml boiling water
10 ml fresh honey
twist of lemon to garnish

Build all ingredients in old-fashioned
glass, finishing with water and honey.
Garnish with twist of lemon.

WHITE NIGHTS

[61]

Martini glass

30 ml vodka
15 ml absinthe
5 ml lime juice
10 ml clear apple juice
slice of lime to garnish

Shake all ingredients except for garnish
with a good scoop of ice. Double-strain
into chilled martini glass and garnish
with slice of lime.

INDIE

DAYDREAM NATION

In a suburban garage near you, an Indie kid is unleashing the beast within. And this animal is not to be tamed: it lusts after distortion, noisy feedback and the kind of sludgy thrash sound belted out by bands such as Mudhoney and Nirvana. This is a sound charmingly defined by an American Indie scene, and proudly recreated by an unequivocal shoe-gazer, who has at some point in his youth treasured Converse sneakers, D.I.Y fanzines and underground radio stations.

Cornerstone anthems like Nirvana's *Smells Like Teen Spirit*, Dinosaur Jr's *Freak Scene* and Sonic Youth's *Dirty Boots*, are to Generation X what Pavement and Band of Horses are to Generation Y latecomers. These are songs defined by nihilism, that scream anti-conformity and charge at the soul like a raging bull on a mission to destroy.

For some it's the slow, heavy drone of The Melvins that best captures Indie, while for others it's the ferocious guitar energy of Sonic Youth that whips the genre. American Indie is just as much about teen angst as it is about churning a virulent punk aggression, finding a loveable pop lick or leaving a mark with an eloquent and distorted riff.

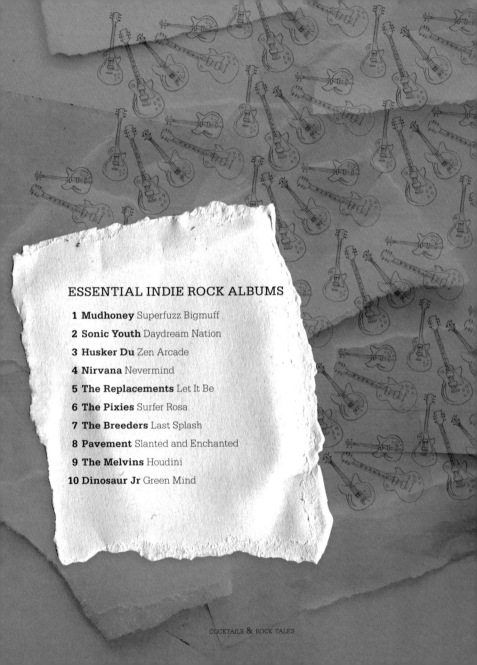

ESSENTIAL INDIE ROCK ALBUMS

1 Mudhoney Superfuzz Bigmuff

2 Sonic Youth Daydream Nation

3 Husker Du Zen Arcade

4 Nirvana Nevermind

5 The Replacements Let It Be

6 The Pixies Surfer Rosa

7 The Breeders Last Splash

8 Pavement Slanted and Enchanted

9 The Melvins Houdini

10 Dinosaur Jr Green Mind

BORDER CROSSING
Martini glass

30 ml tequila
15 ml sloe gin
30 ml fresh lemon juice
30 ml sugar syrup

Shake all ingredients with ice
and strain into a martini glass.

WHISPER

Martini glass

30 ml white rum
30 ml pomegranate liqueur
15 ml lemon juice
45 ml ruby red grapefruit juice
dash of barrel-aged bitters
twist of grapefruit to garnish

Shake all ingredients except for
garnish and double-strain into a
chilled martini glass. Garnish with
twist of grapefruit.

SCURVY DOG
Large beer mug

60 ml cinnamon-infused vodka
15 ml butterscotch schnapps
15 ml orange juice
30 ml soda water
splash of ginger ale
lemon wedge and cherry to garnish

Combine ingredients except for garnish
and shake twice. Pour over ice cubes in
mug and garnish with lemon wedge
and cherry.

BRUNSWICK STREET HUSSY
Highball glass

50 ml gin
10 ml riesling
30 ml lemon juice
15 ml English breakfast tea-infused
  sugar syrup
dash of egg white
English breakfast tea leaves and
  lemon wedge to garnish

Shake all ingredients except for garnish
and strain into highball glass over ice
cubes. Sprinkle with tea leaves and
garnish with lemon wedge.

FEZATINI
Martini glass

30 ml vanilla-infused vodka
10 ml Tuaca
10 ml Licor 43
15 ml Frangelico
15 ml sugar syrup
60 ml espresso coffee
cinnamon sugar to garnish

Combine all ingredients except for
garnish, adding coffee last. Shake
very fast, then strain into martini glass.
Garnish with cinnamon sugar swirls.

HEDONISM
Old-fashioned glass

[67]

1 lime cut into wedges
1 teaspoon brown sugar
30 ml citrus-infused vodka
15 ml Frangelico
15 ml walnut liqueur
extra lime wedge to garnish

Muddle lime and sugar in a mixing glass.
Fill the old-fashioned glass three-quarters
full with ice and add to old-fashioned
glass. Add vodka and liqueurs and top
with shaved ice. Garnish with extra lime
wedge.

SARTRE

Martini glass

30 ml vanilla-infused vodka
15 ml ginger or apple liqueur
10 ml chilli-infused gomme syrup
30 ml cloudy apple juice
3 lime wedges
chilli and lime to garnish

Combine all ingredients except for garnish and shake with ice. Strain into martini glass and garnish with a chilli and twist of lime.

THE SEPARATIST

Wine glass

45 ml amaretto
15 ml cognac
10 ml passionfruit syrup
10 ml vanilla syrup
45 ml cream
grated nutmeg to garnish

Combine amaretto and cognac with the two syrups and steam gently or warm through in a saucepan. Pour into wine glass, layer cream on top and garnish with grated nutmeg.

FALLING CLOUD
Martini glass

45 ml tequila
6 good twists of pepper
25 ml apricot liqueur
15 ml coffee liquor
1 egg yolk
dried apricot to garnish

Combine all ingredients except for garnish. Shake and double-strain into a martini glass and garnish with dried apricot.

FROSTY FRUITS
Martini glass

pulp of 1 fresh passionfruit
(or 4 teaspoons canned
passionfruit pulp)
30 ml gin
30 ml cocoa leaf liqueur
45 ml ruby red grapefruit juice
2 squeezes of lime
orange peel to garnish
(or twist or slice of orange)

Combine all ingredients except for garnish and shake with ice. Double-strain into a chilled martini glass and garnish with orange.

APPLE, CINNAMON, RUM OLD FASHIONED
Old-fashioned glass

1 sugar cube
dash of old-fashioned bitters
15 ml apple liqueur
45 ml rum
orange peel to garnish

Douse sugar cube with bitters in old-fashioned glass and muddle. Add a few cubes of ice and the apple liqueur. Stir to partly dissolve ingredients. Top with half the rum. Add ice and stir. Add remaining rum and more ice. Garnish with squeezed orange peel.

THE CRACK FOX
Martini glass

2 strawberries
2 watermelon chunks
50 ml gin
10 ml black raspberry liqueur
20 ml pineapple juice
cracked black pepper to garnish

Muddle fruit in shaker. Add all remaining
ingredients except for garnish and
shake vigorously. Double-strain into
martini glass and garnish with cracked
black pepper.

BLAST OFF

Old-fashioned glass

4 coriander leaves
6 mint sprigs
½ lime, roughly chopped
1 teaspoon palm sugar
30 ml chilli-infused vodka
15 ml kaffir lime-
    and lemongrass-infused vodka
15 ml coconut rum
extra coriander leaves and chilli
    to garnish

Muddle coriander, mint, lime and sugar
in mixing glass. Add vodkas and coconut
rum and shake with crushed ice. Pour into
old-fashioned glass. Top with crushed
ice and garnish with coriander leaves
and chilli.

CLAMPDOWN

Old-fashioned glass

½ pear, roughly chopped
1 teaspoon vanilla sugar
45 ml vanilla-infused vodka
15 ml pear liqueur
soda water

Muddle pear and vanilla sugar in shaker.
Add vodka and pear liquor and shake
briefly with crushed ice. Pour into old-
fashioned glass and top with soda
to taste.

KOO KOO KACHOO
Martini glass

30 ml smoky single malt Scotch whisky
30 ml grappa
20 ml Licor 43
2 slices fresh apple
dash of orange bitters
twist of grapefruit to garnish

Stir all ingredients except for garnish
and double-strain into martini glass.
Garnish with twist of grapefruit.

ENLYTENMINT
Pilsner glass

8 blueberries
5 mint leaves
½ lime,
30 ml lychee pulp
30 ml black raspberry liqueur
30 ml tequila
splash of ginger beer
orchid flower, lime wedge and fresh
**   lychee to garnish**

Muddle the blueberries, mint, lime and
lychee pulp with the liqueur and tequila.
Shake well and pour into pilsner glass.
Top up with ginger beer. Garnish with
orchid, lime wedge and lychee.

SHOT TOWER

Sling glass

1 sugar cube
10 ml absinthe
20 ml amaretto
20 ml French vermouth
20 ml vodka
30 ml lime juice
splash of lemonade

Place sugar cube on absinthe spoon
and sit on top of glass, Pour absinthe
onto sugar cube and ignite. Once sugar
cube has dissolved drop it into glass and
discard spoon. Combine all remaining
ingredients except lemonade in a shaker.
Add ice and shake then pour into glass.
Top up with lemonade.

INDIE DAYDREAM NATION

ODE TO PERSEVERANCE
Wine glass

50 ml tequila
10 ml yellow Chartreuse
3 basil leaves
20 ml lime juice
dash of egg white
10 ml honey
1 extra basil leaf to garnish

Shake ingredients then double-
strain into chilled wine glass.
Garnish with extra basil leaf.

MOSCOVITE MUSCATEER

Coupette glass

45 ml vodka
10 ml muscat
30 ml cranberry juice
1 teaspoon lemon curd

Shake all ingredients then double-strain
into coupette glass.

IN A PICKLE
Martini glass

splash of Jägermeister
60 ml vodka
slice of cornichon to garnish

Add a splash of Jägermeister to
chilled martini glass and swirl to coat.
Combine vodka with ice in a mixing
glass. Stir and double-strain into
martini glass. Spear cornichon slice
with a toothpick and use to garnish.

FUNKY MIDNIGHT
Colada glass

45 ml peach schnapps
15 ml blue curaçao
5 ml grenadine syrup
splash of soda water
splash of lemonade
maraschino cherry to garnish

Fill colada glass a third full with ice.
Build schnapps, blue curaçao and
grenadine in glass and swirl to mix.
Top up carefully with half each of
lemonade and soda water, forming
a deep purple base that thins to a clear
top. Garnish with maraschino cherry.

BLOODY BRUSSELS
Highball glass

chilli flakes
sesame seeds
celery salt
30 ml chilli-infused vodka
10 ml garlic-infused vodka
15 ml lemon juice
60 ml tomato juice
10 ml Worcestershire sauce
dash of balsamic vinegar
extra celery salt to season
cracked pepper to season
long stick of celery, long stick of
   cucumber and lemon slice to garnish

Moisten rim of highball glass and coat
with chilli flakes, sesame seeds and
celery salt.

Build remaining ingredients in glass,
except for garnish, and stir. Garnish with
celery cucumber and lemon slice.

BRAMBLE
Martini glass

30 ml gin
30 ml black raspberry liqueur
15 ml lemon juice
30 ml sugar syrup

Shake all ingredients with ice and strain into martini glass.

ORANGE ALL ROUND
Wine glass

30 ml whisky
30 ml fresh orange juice
10 ml peach liqueur
10 ml maraschino liqueur
dash of orange bitters
1 egg yolk
twist of orange to garnish

Shake ingredients well and double-strain into orange sugar-crusted wine glass. Garnish with twist of orange.

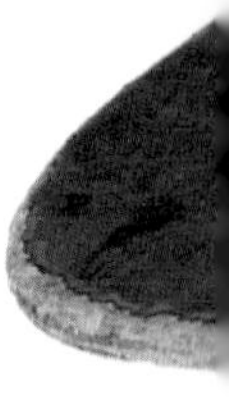

CHOCOLATE AND CHILLI MARTINI
Martini glass

60 ml vodka
30 ml dark crème de cacao
1 bird's eye chilli, sliced
1 extra chilli to garnish

Combine all ingredients except for
garnish then shake and double-strain into
chilled martini glass. Garnish with extra
chilli on rim of glass.

TRY A LITTLE TENDERNESS

Born from a place both divine and earthly, nothing tugs at the heartstrings like Soul music. Recording artists from the 1950s, such as Sam Cooke, Ray Charles and James Brown, invented the wheel that keeps spinning in Soul's glory. These music legends captured Soul's courteous essence by bringing Gospel, Pop and R & B to the table in a unified handshake. Songs like Sam Cooke's *You Send Me*, James Brown's *Papa's Got A Brand New Bag* and Ray Charles' *I Believe To My Soul* are cornerstones of a genre that nurtures matters of the heart and a belief in self-assertion.

There's a mighty strength to the hardships one feels through soul music. And it doesn't just begin and end with love gone wrong – even though many Soul songs resonate loudly with the broken-hearted. In fact, the sound of Soul was built on a sexy rebellion: one that was steeped in themes of racial emancipation and religion, economic hardships and geographical remoteness.

The tough armoury of soul is not entirely too hot to handle, but it's exactly this hard-to-crack charm that wins many people over to its cause. Soul may have risen from the disadvantaged corner of Black American culture, but through its sorrowful roots it delivers a sweet sound that brings hope to the many who embrace her warmth.

TOP 10 SOUL SONGS

1 **Ray Charles** I Believe To My Soul

2 **Irma Thomas** Of My Heart

3 **Sam Cooke** A Change Is Gonna Come

4 **The Impressions** People Get Ready

5 **James Brown**
Papa's Got A Brand New Bag

6 **Betty Lavette** Let Me Down Easy

7 **Otis Redding** Try A Little Tenderness

8 **Lee Moses** Bad Girl (Part 1)

9 **Bobby Bland**
Rockin' In The Same Old Boat

10 **Mavis Staples** Since I Fell For You

B.B. KING
Martini glass

5 ml absinthe
5 ml sugar syrup
30 ml bourbon
30 ml brandy or cognac
3 dashes of bitters
twist of lemon to garnish

Swirl absinthe and sugar syrup around
in martini glass. Combine all remaining
ingredients except for garnish and stir
with ice. Strain into martini glass and
garnish with twist of lemon.

BROWN SUGAR [85]
Highball glass

juice of 1 lime
1 teaspoon brown sugar
45 ml dark rum
15 ml white rum
10 ml Licor 43
dash of bitters
splash of cola
wedge of lime and mint sprig
**   to garnish**

Muddle lime juice and sugar in shaker
until dissolved. Add all remaining
ingredients except cola and garnish and
shake with ice. Strain into highball glass
over ice. Top up with cola and garnish
with lime wedge and mint sprig.

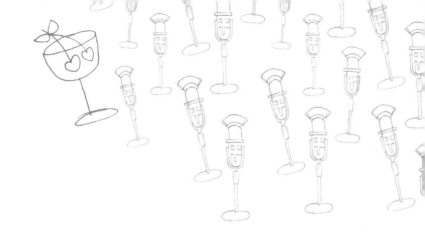

PEAR FONDUE
Martini glass

30 ml vodka
20 ml pear liqueur
10 ml crème de cacao
3 chocolate-coated coffee beans
**   to garnish**

Shake all ingredients except for garnish
then double-strain through a tea strainer
into chilled martini glass. Garnish with 3
chocolate-coated coffee beans.

GINGER ZING
Martini glass

60 ml potato vodka
5 ml ginger liqueur
splash of chilli-infused vodka
slice of fresh ginger
julienne of fresh ginger to garnish

Stir all ingredients except for garnish in a
mixing glass then double-strain through
a tea strainer into chilled martini glass.
Garnish with julienne of fresh ginger.

BONGO BEAT
Colada glass

30 ml peach vodka
15 ml kiwi-infused vodka
15 ml passionfruit-infused vodka
60 ml guava nectar
30 ml pineapple juice
30 ml passionfruit pulp
juice of ½ lime
dash of coconut syrup
pineapple wedge to garnish

Build all ingredients except for garnish
over ice and stir. Garnish with pineapple
wedge and stalk.

VINCENT'S NIGHT CAFÉ
Martini glass

45 ml vodka
15 ml absinthe
5 ml green Charteuse
bruised mint leaf to garnish

Stir all ingredients except for garnish in
a mixing glass then strain into martini
glass. Garnish with bruised mint leaf.

TU MADRE

Martini glass

2 red chillies
2 cm x 2 cm piece fresh ginger, roughly
  chopped
45 ml tequila
15 ml Licor 43
30 ml lemon juice
1 ½ teaspoons honey
1 extra chilli to garnish

Muddle chillies and ginger in shaker.
Add all remaining ingredients except for
garnish and stir to dissolve honey. Add
ice and shake. Double-strain into martini
glass and garnish with chilli.

FAIR LADY

Martini glass

½ pink lady apple, roughly chopped
1 rambutan
45 ml gin
15 ml pear liqueur
splash of rosewater
1 extra rambutan, half-peeled,
  to garnish

Muddle apple and rambutan in shaker.
Add all remaining ingredients except for
garnish and shake. Strain into martini
glass and garnish with half-peeled
rambutan on rim of glass.

LADY MARMALADE
Hurricane glass

45 ml gin
30 ml lemon juice
15 ml sugar syrup
1 heaped teaspoon marmalade
splash of tonic water
slices of orange, lemon and lime
**   to garnish**

Combine all ingredients except for
tonic water and garnish in shaker.
Shake vigorously and strain into
hurricane glass over ice. Top up with
tonic water and garnish with orange,
lemon and lime slices.

RESPECT
Martini glass

3 slivers peach
45 ml vanilla vodka
30 ml crème de pêches
orchid flower to garnish

Muddle peach slivers in shaker.
Add vodka and crème de pêches
and shake with ice. Double-strain
into chilled martini glass and garnish
with orchid flower.

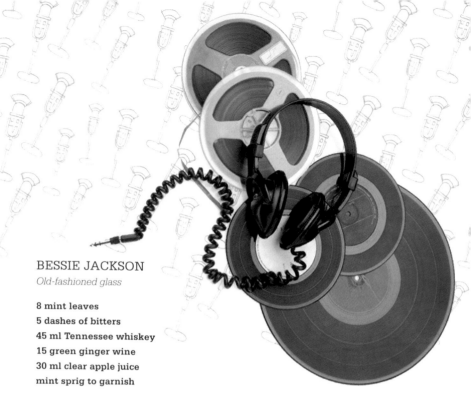

BESSIE JACKSON
Old-fashioned glass

8 mint leaves
5 dashes of bitters
45 ml Tennessee whiskey
15 green ginger wine
30 ml clear apple juice
mint sprig to garnish

Muddle mint leaves and bitters in shaker.
Add all remaining ingredients except for
garnish and shake with ice. Double-strain
into old-fashioned glass over ice and
garnish with mint sprig.

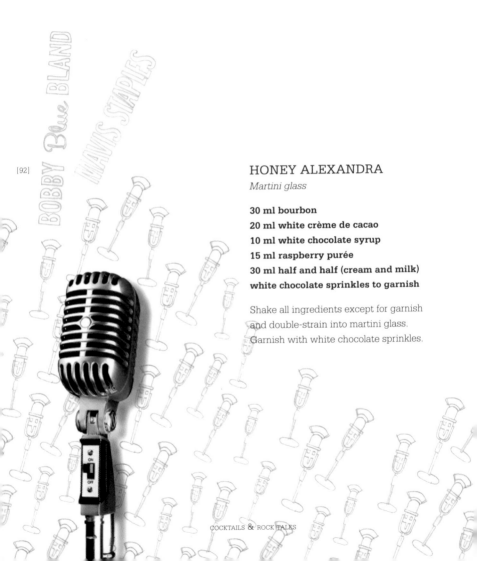

HONEY ALEXANDRA
Martini glass

30 ml bourbon
20 ml white crème de cacao
10 ml white chocolate syrup
15 ml raspberry purée
30 ml half and half (cream and milk)
white chocolate sprinkles to garnish

Shake all ingredients except for garnish
and double-strain into martini glass.
Garnish with white chocolate sprinkles.

LIMESTONE MARTINI
Martini glass

2 cm piece cucumber, roughly chopped
60 ml gin
15 ml lime juice
15 ml gomme syrup
1 egg white
julienne of cucumber to garnish

Shake all ingredients except for garnish
and double-strain into martini glass. Float
cucumber julienne to garnish.

TOASTED HAZELNUT
AND CHOC TREACLE

Large old-fashioned glass

30 ml rum
20 ml chocolate liqueur
10 ml Frangelico
5 ml orgeat syrup
flamed hazelnut essence to garnish
atomiser filled with overproof rum

Build in old-fashioned glass. Garnish with
flamed hazelnut essence and spray with
overproof rum.

LADY KILLER

Champagne flute

3 strawberries
15 ml vodka
15 ml black raspberry liqueur
dash of sugar syrup
splash of prosecco

Muddle strawberries in shaker. Add
vodka, liqueur and sugar syrup and shake.
Double-strain into flute over prosecco

MOJITO REVOLUTION

Highball glass

8–10 mint leaves
45 ml rum
30 ml guava juice
30 ml lime juice
10 ml caramel syrup
dash orange bitters
splash of soda water
extra mint sprig to garnish

Combine all ingredients except for
garnish in highball glass. Fill with ice and
stir. Garnish with mint sprig.

MANDARIN SIDECAR

[95]

Large martini glass

½ lemon, roughly chopped
45 ml brandy
15 ml mandarin liqueur
flamed orange zest to garnish

Muddle lemon in shaker. Add brandy
and liqueur and shake. Double-strain
into a large martini glass with a brown
sugar-encrusted rim. Garnish with flamed
orange zest.

SMOKEY HONEY MARTINI
Martini glass

5–10 ml smoky Scotch whisky
60 ml vodka
5 ml honey
piece of honeycomb to garnish

Swirl whisky around in martini
glass and discard any excess.
Shake vodka with honey and
double-strain into glass. Garnish
with honeycomb

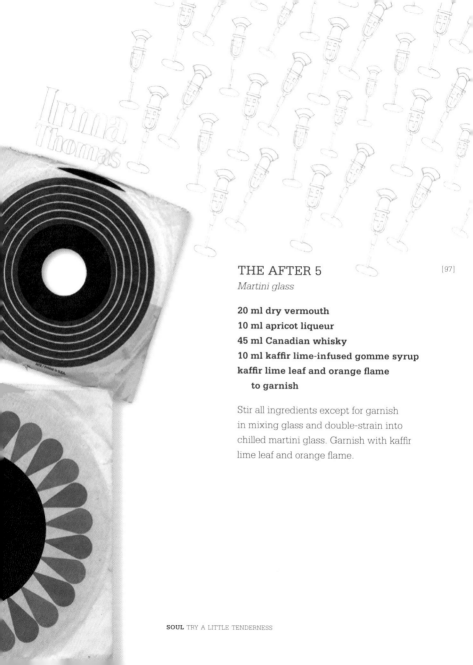

THE AFTER 5 [97]
Martini glass

20 ml dry vermouth
10 ml apricot liqueur
45 ml Canadian whisky
10 ml kaffir lime-infused gomme syrup
kaffir lime leaf and orange flame
    to garnish

Stir all ingredients except for garnish
in mixing glass and double-strain into
chilled martini glass. Garnish with kaffir
lime leaf and orange flame.

DA RENAGADE
Old-fashioned glass

45 ml tequila
90 ml sweet and sour mix
dash of Tuaca

Shake tequila and sweet and sour
mix with ice 'til all shook up, and
dump into old-fashioned glass. Float
a dash of Tuaca on top.

SULTANAS OF SWING
Highball glass

1 tablespoon rye whisky-soaked
  sultanas
50 ml tequila
10 ml Benedictine
2 dashes of bitters
30 ml lemon juice
15 ml sugar syrup
dash of egg white
grated nutmeg and orange zest
  to garnish

Muddle sultanas in shaker. Add all remaining ingredients except for garnish and shake with ice. Strain into highball glass over ice. Garnish with nutmeg and orange zest.

GONZALES
Martini glass

½ lemon, roughly chopped
½ lime, roughly chopped
30 ml tequila
30 ml Grand Marnier
15 ml apple liqueur
3 drops of orange bitters

Muddle lemon and lime in shaker. Add remaining ingredients and shake with ice. Strain into martini glass with cinnamon-sugar-encrusted rim.

Noir

BLOODLETTING

We all like to channel the dark side on occasion. Noir can be
the ideal hideaway when life feels extreme. Swimming in its
depths brings everyone from Swans, The Birthday Party,
Nick Cave and The Bad Seeds and Ministry to the poolside
of our emotional destruction, and it is the 'upper' we need
when things seem bleak.

But there is hope in Noir's pessimism, despite its morbid
evanescence. Sometimes it's the post-industrial sounds that
soothe the soul, while for others, it's Noir's eternal nihilism that
somehow helps tweak a smile.

Swans capture Noir through hypnotic beats and dark ambient
sounds while The Birthday Party revel in a blood-letting
atypical of the avant-Noir scene. Elsewhere, there's
Einsturzende Neubaten's distinctive drilling massacre of sounds,
Nick Cave's bloodthirsty poetry, Lydia Lunch's self-professing
anger, Nine Inch Nails' razor-sharp industrialism and Mark
Lanegan and The Gutter Twins' self-loathing and redemption
– all of which footnote Noir and hide behind her morbid veil.

These dark horses and heiresses trot through the fields of despair
and show us the bleakness of life's woes. Noir is moody. It's dark,
gothic, fragile, cinematic and intense – and nothing is quite as
narcotic as the music it spawns.

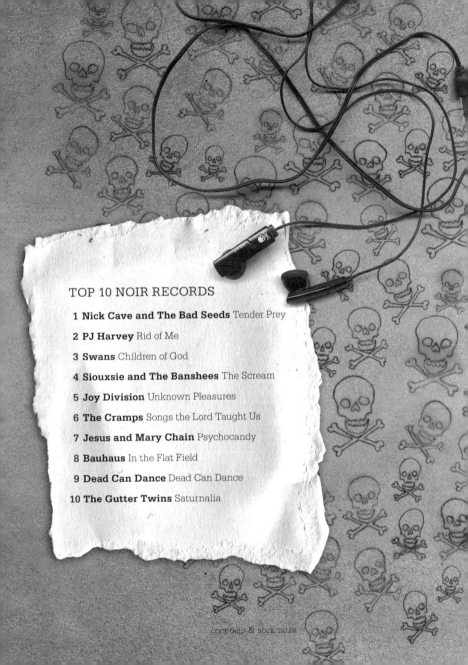

TOP 10 NOIR RECORDS

1 **Nick Cave and The Bad Seeds** Tender Prey

2 **PJ Harvey** Rid of Me

3 **Swans** Children of God

4 **Siouxsie and The Banshees** The Scream

5 **Joy Division** Unknown Pleasures

6 **The Cramps** Songs the Lord Taught Us

7 **Jesus and Mary Chain** Psychocandy

8 **Bauhaus** In the Flat Field

9 **Dead Can Dance** Dead Can Dance

10 **The Gutter Twins** Saturnalia

FLOATING SNOW
Highball glass

30 ml vodka
15 ml limoncello
3 dashes of bitters
30 ml lemon juice
8 mint leaves
splash of apple juice
extra mint sprig to garnish

Shake all ingredients except for
apple juice and garnish, and strain
into highball over ice cubes. Top with
apple juice and garnish with mint sprig.

OBLIVIOUS
Martini glass

45 ml Aperol
15 ml pomarancza vodka
15 ml blood orange juice
15 ml lemon juice
30 ml egg white
maraschino cherry to garnish

Shake all ingredients except for
garnish and pour into martini glass.
Garnish with maraschino cherry.

SILENT ROSE
Old-fashioned glass

½ **kiwi fruit**
10 ml rose syrup
30 ml pineapple
   and guava-infused vodka
15 ml Aperol
20 ml lemon juice
dash of egg white
3 lemon slices to garnish

Muddle the kiwifruit and syrup then add all other ingredients. Shake with ice

and strain into an old-fashioned glass over ice. Garnish with lemon slices.

BURNT ORANGE MANHATTAN
Large martini glass

zest of ½ orange
5 ml cognac
dash of bitters
30 ml rye whiskey
15 ml sweet vermouth
15 ml dry vermouth

In a mixing glass burn orange zest with cognac until flame dies. Reserve half flamed zest to garnish. Add bitters, whisky and vermouths to remainder and stir well. Double-strain into a large martini glass and garnish with flamed orange zest.

MAIL ORDER BRIDE
Martini glass

2 cm piece chopped fresh ginger
pinch of white pepper
sprinkle of grated cinnamon
sprinkle of grated nutmeg
45 ml apple vodka
15 ml port
15 ml vanilla syrup
15 ml lemon juice
3 apple slices to garnish

Muddle the ginger, pepper, cinnamon and nutmeg in a shaker. Add all the remaining ingredients except for garnish and shake well. Double-strain into martini glass and garnish with apple slices.

CONQUETE
Highball glass

30 ml ml white rum
30 ml cloudy apple juice
10 ml black raspberry liqueur
10 ml passionfruit liqueur
1 teaspoon raspberry purée
10 ml strawberry liqueur
3 wedges of lime to garnish

Build over highball with ice. Drizzle raspberry purée over ice then top with strawberry liqueur. Garnish with lime wedges.

MILLS AND BOON
Martini glass

30 ml citrus-infused vodka
30 ml Cointreau
30 ml cloudy apple juice
3 wedges of lime
10–15 ml blood orange juice
twist of orange to garnish

Combine all ingredients except for garnish and shake with ice. Strain into martini glass and garnish with orange flame and twist.

UNTITLED #3
Martini glass

4–5 chunks of fresh cucumber
(about 2 x 2cm)
¾ – 1 small red chilli (to taste)
6–7 fresh coriander leaves
45 ml gin
15 ml Licor 43
1 teaspoon green Chartreuse
small squeeze of lemon
coriander leaf to garnish

Muddle cucumber well then add chilli and coriander and muddle again briefly. Add all the remaining ingredients except for garnish and shake vigorously with ice. Double-strain into a chilled martini glass and garnish with a floating coriander leaf.

SISTER MILLER
Collins glass

45 ml bourbon
15 ml crème de cacao
15 ml lemon juice
15 ml cloudy apple juice

Shake all ingredients with ice. Strain into a collins glass over ice.

BLOOD AND SAND
Martini glass

30 ml whisky
15 ml dry vermouth
15 ml cherry liqueur
15 ml orange juice
15 ml lemon juice
dash of sugar syrup

Shake all ingredients together and double-strain into martini glass.

RED SNAPPER
Highball glass

60 ml gin
100 ml tomato juice
10 ml lemon juice
salt
pepper
1 teaspoon wasabi paste
dash of Worcestershire sauce and
cucumber slice to garnish

Combine all ingredients except for
garnish in a shaker with ice. Strain
into highball glass over ice. Add a dash
of Worcestershire sauce and garnish
with cucumber.

CONSTANCE STREET
Wine glass

whisky to rinse
45 ml cognac
15 ml cherry liqueur
15 ml port
5 ml cinnamon-infused gomme syrup
dash of bitters
orange zest to garnish

Rinse wine glass with whisky and dip glass rim into sugar until thickly en-crusted.

Shake all remaining ingredients except for garnish and double-strain into wine glass over ice cubes. Garnish with orange zest.

RAISON D'ETRE
Martini glass

45 ml Tennessee whiskey
15 ml Licor 43
20 ml pear juice
10 ml lime juice
10 ml raisin- and chilli-infused
  sugar syrup
stemmed dried muscatels to garnish

Combine all ingredients except for
garnish and shake with ice. Double-
strain into martini glass. Garnish with
dried muscatels.

CAFFE SOCIETY MARTINI [111]
Martini glass

15 ml vanilla-infused vodka
15 ml Licor 43
15 ml Kahlúa Especiale
15 ml Grand Marnier
shot of espresso, chilled

Shake all ingredients vigorously and
strain into martini glass.

SAZERAC DE LOUIS
Old-fashioned glass

dash of absinthe
45 ml cognac
10 ml sugar syrup
3 dashes of bitters
orange rind and twist of orange
    to garnish

Chill old-fashioned glass with ice. Rinse
with absinthe then discard. Combine
cognac, sugar syrup and bitters in a
shaker. Shake and double-strain into
old-fashioned glass. Squeeze orange
rind and rub rim of glass with citrus oil.
Garnish with twist of orange.

MA CHERIE
Colada glass

45 ml gin
15 ml cherry liqueur
splash of lime juice
splash of lemon juice
1 sugar cube
splash of maraschino cherry juice
splash of soda water
2 lime wedges to garnish

Combine all ingredients except for cherry
juice soda and garnish. Strain into colada
glass over ice cubes. Top with cherry
juice and soda to taste and garnish with
lime wedges.

MAC-TRINIDADDY
Brandy balloon

30 ml rum
5 ml amaretto
15 ml honey liqueur
30 ml lime juice
10 ml Earl Grey tea-infused
    sugar syrup
dash of orange bitters
dash of egg white
mint sprig and Earl Grey tea leaves
    to garnish

Combine all ingredients except for garnish in a shaker. Shake well and double-strain into brandy balloon over crushed ice. Garnish with mint sprig and Earl Grey tea leaves.

[114] BEETROOT AND VANILLA MOJITO
Highball glass

8 mint leaves
6 cubes diced canned beetroot
50 ml white rum
30 ml lime juice
15 ml vanilla-infused sugar syrup
5 ml Licor 43
splash of soda water
mint sprig to garnish

Rub mint leaves around rim of highball glass then drop them in. Muddle with beetroot. Add all remaining liquids, except for soda water, then fill glass with crushed ice. Stir well then top up with soda water. Top with crushed ice and garnish with mint sprig.

PASSION FOR THE CHRISTCHURCH

Collins glass

30 ml gin
15 ml Campari
15 ml lemon juice
45 ml ruby grapefruit juice
10 ml sugar syrup
pulp of ½ passionfruit

Shake all ingredients and strain into collins glass over ice. Garnish with spent passionfruit shell.

GIMLET VIA BORGANES

Martini glass

handful diced fresh pineapple
60 ml gin
15 ml lime juice
10 ml orange syrup
cracked black pepper
long cucumber 'chopsticks'

Muddle pineapple. Add liquids, and
shake. Double-strain into martini glass
and garnish with cracked black pepper
and cucumber chopsticks.

C TO THE CIROC
Martini glass

5 green grapes
60 ml vodka
dash peach liqueur
30 ml apple juice
15 ml sauvignon blanc
small bunch of grapes to garnish

Muddle grapes in shaker. Add all
remaining ingredients except for garnish
and shake. Double-strain into chilled
martini glass and garnish with a small
bunch of grapes.

CARAJILLO MARTINI
Martini glass

[117]

30 ml espresso coffee
30 ml vodka
15 ml Pedro Ximenez sherry
10 ml black raspberry liqueur
10 ml vanilla-infused gomme syrup
freshly grated nutmeg and cinnamon
    powder to garnish

Combine all ingredients except for
garnish in shaker. Shake vigorously
with ice. Strain into a martini glass
and garnish with freshly grated nutmeg
and cinnamon.

PENULTIMATE SUPPER

Sling glass

3 chunks melon
45 ml rum
10 ml lemon juice
10 ml Grand Marnier
Champagne or sparkling wine
strip of melon peel to garnish

Combine melon chunks, rum, lemon juice
and Grand Marnier in shaker. Shake well
and strain into sling glass over ice. Top
with bubbles and garnish with strip of
melon peel

RUSSIAN DOUBLE AGENT

Large old-fashioned glass

30 ml espresso coffee
30 ml Tia Maria
dash of sugar syrup
30 ml cream
30 ml vodka
3 coffee beans to garnish

Combine espresso, Tia Maria and sugar
syrup in one shaker. Combine cream and
vodka in another shaker. Shake both then
strain coffee mix over ice into large old-
fashioned glass. Layer cream mix on top
and garnish with coffee beans.

FOGCUTTER
Tiki mug

60 ml rum
30 ml cognac
15 ml gin
45 ml lemon juice
30 ml orange juice
15 ml orgeat syrup
10 ml Pedro Ximenez sherry

Shake all ingredients, except for PX
sherry, and strain into tiki mug over ice.
Float PX sherry on top.

Psychedelic

FLASHBACK

Psychedelic is for those who don't seek the bleeding obvious, for here exists a sound bent on taking you on a spaced-out journey, fuelled by flighty tangents that lead you into a world of freak-out.

But the whimsical fairytale energy of Psychedelic is deliberate. It couldn't smell more 'real' than the Small Faces' *Ogden's Nut Gone Flake* recorded in 1968 – even though the album is charged with hallucinatory effects and instrumental diversions.

It was dreamy Psychedelic hits such as *Slip Inside This House* and *You're Gonna Miss Me* from Roky Erickson and his 13th Floor Elevators (Janis Joplin even considered joining this group in the 1960s) that captured the true essence of the genre. Mind-altering substances may have assisted Erickson in unlocking the door to his other-worldly experiences, and it was these diversions that gave birth to his Psychedelic trip.

Even the Beatles found Psychedelic comforting; think of their trippy song *Lucy In The Sky With Diamonds*. Ted Nugget was a pioneer of sorts, bringing together '60s Garage with 'primitive fuzz' and even Jerry Garcia from the Grateful Dead left a mark on Psychedelic by plugging into its demented sound. The late Timothy Leary may have advocated the 'turn on, tune in and drop out' philosophy, but it was Psychedelic music that really embraced his motto.

TOP 10 PSYCHEDELIC RECORDS

1 **Small Faces** Ogden's Nut Gone Flake

2 **Ted Nugget** Original Artyfacts From
The First Psychedelic Era 1965-1968

3 **13th Floor Elevators** Easter Everywhere

4 **Grateful Dead** Aoxomoxoa

5 **Jimi Hendrix** Axis: Bold As Love

6 **The Beatles** Sgt. Pepper's Lonely Hearts
Club Band

7 **The Moving Sidewalks** Flash

8 **The Beach Boys** Pet Sounds

9 **Hawkwind** Space Ritual

10 **Pink Floyd** A Saucerful Of Secrets

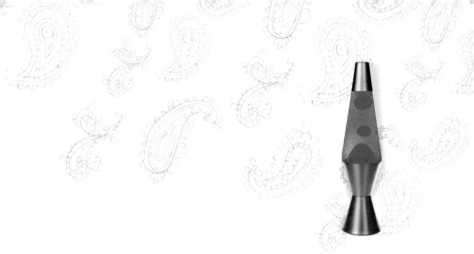

KAT KILLER
Martini glass

30 ml lemon-infused vodka
15 ml peach liqueur
30 ml apple juice
30 ml ruby red grapefruit juice
flamed orange zest to garnish

Shake all ingredients with ice. Strain into chilled martini glass. Rub the rim of the glass with the flamed orange zest and float to garnish.

ZSA ZSA'S FLOWER

Martini glass

juice of 1 lime
30 ml gin
15 ml Aperol
15 ml Licor 43
splash of pink grapefruit juice
white orchid to garnish

Muddle lime in shaker. Add all remaining ingredients except for garnish. Shake and strain into martini glass. Garnish with a white orchid.

PANG'S PUNCH
Pint glass

45 ml coconut rum
20 ml light rum
15 ml blue curaçao
90 ml pineapple juice
splash of soda water
slice of pineapple, maraschino cherry
**   and glow stick to garnish**

Fill shaker with ice. Add both rums and
shake twice, then pour into pint glass.
Stir in blue curaçao and pineapple juice
and a splash of soda. Garnish with
pineapple, cherry and glow stick.

THE JAZZ
Highball glass

½ orange, roughly chopped
1 teaspoon brown sugar
45 ml single malt Scotch whisky
6 mint leaves
splash of soda water
10 ml Tia Maria
sprig of mint to garnish

Muddle orange with brown sugar in
shaker. Add whisky. Tear and smack the
mint leaves 2–3 times and add to shaker.
Fill three-quarters full with crushed ice
then shake well. Pour into highball glass.
Top with soda and drizzle on Tia Maria.
Garnish with a sprig of mint.

TINI DE BLACKBERRY
Martini glass

60 ml gin
10 drops crème de mûres

Pour gin into chilled martini glass.
Add 5 drops of crème de mûres and
stir. Double- strain the ingredients.
Add another 5 drops of crème de
mûres so that they sink to the bottom
of the glass.

ORANGE ZESTINI
Martini glass

60 ml gin
½ teaspoon dry vermouth
½ teaspoon orange bitters
oil from orange rind
thick twist of orange

Combine gin, vermouth and bitters in
mixing glass with ice. Stir and double-
strain into chilled martini glass. Squeeze
the orange rind thoroughly over the entire
surface of the drink, saturating it with
citrus oil. Twist the thick orange garnish
onto drink and float.

BOB MARLEY PUNCH
Colada glass

30 ml rum
15 ml honey-infused vodka
15 ml vanilla-infused vodka
30 ml mango nectar
30 ml pineapple juice
30 ml passionfruit pulp
¼ fresh mango
juice of ½ lime
dash of coconut syrup
slice mango to garnish

Blend all ingredients except for garnish at high speed with a scoop of ice. Pour into colada glass and garnish with mango slice.

ROAST CAPSICUM AND WHITE CHOCOLATE MARGARITA
Martini glass

2 slithers roasted red capsicum
60 ml tequila
30 ml white crème de cacao
30 ml lime juice
lemon pepper to garnish rim

Muddle roasted capsicum in shaker. Add remaining ingredients except for garnish and shake. Double-strain into chilled martini glass. Garnish rim of glass with lemon pepper.

HENDRICK'S 75
Champagne flute

5 cm piece cucumber
10 ml elderflower syrup
20 ml Hendrick's gin
sparkling wine to taste

Muddle cucumber in shaker. Add
all remaining ingredients except for
sparkling wine and shake. Double-strain
into champagne flute over sparkling wine.

SAZERAC
Old-fashioned glass

5 ml absinthe
30 ml cognac
30 ml rye bourbon
2 drops of bitters
2 drops of orange bitters
10 ml gomme syrup

Fill old-fashioned glass with water and
stir in absinthe. Set aside. Combine
remaining ingredients in mixing glass and
stir well. Discard absinthe and water and
strain drink into the coated glass.

WATERMELON MAN
Martini glass

1 cm piece of fresh ginger
6–8 mint leaves
45 ml rum
15 ml watermelon liqueur
10 ml gingembre liqueur
watermelon balls to garnish

Muddle all ingredients except for garnish in shaker. Add ice then shake and double-strain into martini glass. Garnish with watermelon balls on skewer.

PSYCHEDELIC FLASHBACK

SPACE ODDITY NO.9
Highball glass

30 ml cranberry-infused vodka
10 ml Tuaca
10 ml black raspberry liqueur
60 ml apple juice
15 ml raspberry purée

Shake all ingredients with ice until
spacey. Strain into highball glass.

PURPLE HAZE

Large old-fashioned glass

4 lime wedges
15 ml violette syrup
4–5 mint leaves
45 ml vanilla-infused vodka
10 ml honey liqueur
10 ml apple juice
30 ml ginger beer
mint sprig or mint leaves to garnish

Muddle lime and syrup in shaker.
Add ice and all remaining ingredients,
except ginger beer and garnish. Shake
briefly but vigorously, then double-strain
into a large old-fashioned glass three-
quarters filled with ice. Add ginger beer
and stir briefly. Top with cubed or crushed
ice and garnish with mint sprigs or
fanned mint leaves.

POMEGRANATE SLING

[131]

Highball glass

2 star anise
½ fresh lemon, roughly chopped
45 ml dry gin
10 ml Benedictine
60 ml pomegranate juice
10 ml sugar syrup
15 ml pomegranate liqueur
soda water
several star anise and pomegranate
  seeds to garnish

Smash star anise in shaker. Add
lemon and muddle. Add all remaining
ingredients, except for soda water and
garnish, and shake well. Double-strain
into highball glass over ice. Top with soda
and stir. Garnish with extra star anise and
pomegranate seeds.

PEANUT BUTTER FLIP
Martini glass

45 ml white rum
10 ml sugar syrup
10 ml Licor 43
2 teaspoons peanut butter
2 teaspoons cream
1 egg yolk

Shake ingredients vigorously and double-strain into martini glass.

T-LAM-CHI
Pilsner glass

½ fresh lime, roughly chopped
30 ml tequila
30 ml sour apple schnapps
20 ml lychee pulp
5 ml kiwi fruit syrup
fresh mint leaves
splash of sparkling mineral water
slice of kiwi fruit and cherries
**   to garnish**

Muddle lime in shaker. Add all remaining ingredients except for sparkling water and garnish and shake well. Pour into pilsner glass and top with sparkling water. Garnish with slice of kiwi and cherries.

SMALL FACES

POISON AIVY

[133]

Martini glass

2 strawberries
45 ml Aivy vodka
15 ml Licor 43
30 ml cranberry juice
15 ml guava juice
2 squeezes of lemon
strawberry cut into flower shape
    to garnish

Muddle strawberries in shaker. Add all remaining ingredients except for garnish and shake with ice. Double-strain into chilled martini glass and garnish with strawberry flower.

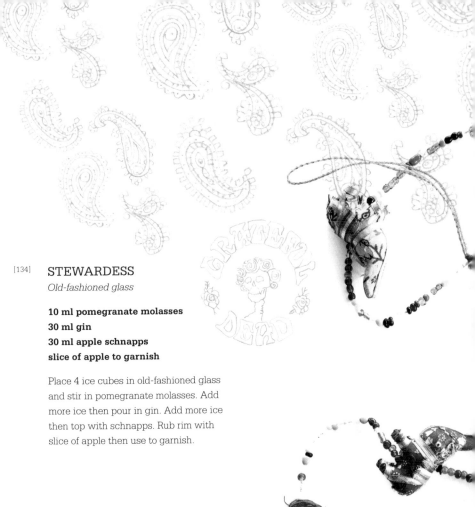

STEWARDESS
Old-fashioned glass

10 ml pomegranate molasses
30 ml gin
30 ml apple schnapps
slice of apple to garnish

Place 4 ice cubes in old-fashioned glass
and stir in pomegranate molasses. Add
more ice then pour in gin. Add more ice
then top with schnapps. Rub rim with
slice of apple then use to garnish.

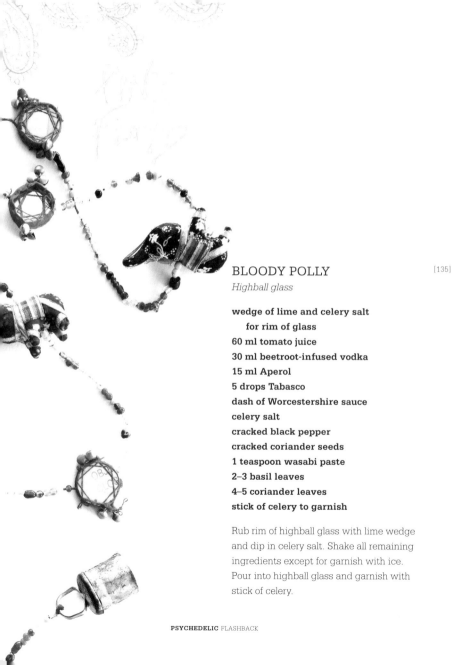

BLOODY POLLY

Highball glass

wedge of lime and celery salt
for rim of glass
60 ml tomato juice
30 ml beetroot-infused vodka
15 ml Aperol
5 drops Tabasco
dash of Worcestershire sauce
celery salt
cracked black pepper
cracked coriander seeds
1 teaspoon wasabi paste
2–3 basil leaves
4–5 coriander leaves
stick of celery to garnish

Rub rim of highball glass with lime wedge
and dip in celery salt. Shake all remaining
ingredients except for garnish with ice.
Pour into highball glass and garnish with
stick of celery.

PSYCHEDELIC FLASHBACK

DR GONZO
Martini glass

2 lime wedges, halved
10 ml vanilla-infused sugar syrup
10 ml apricot syrup
30 ml Tuaca
30 ml dark rum
30 ml cranberry juice
cardamom seeds to garnish

Muddle lime wedges with syrups.
Shake with ice then pour into martini
glass. Stir in remaining ingredients and
garnish with cardamon seeds.

NASTY MARTINI
Martini glass

10 ml orange syrup
20 ml vodka
20 ml Grand Marnier
15 ml absinthe
orange zest to garnish
splash of orange juice to serve

Rub rim of cocktail glass with orange syrup. Combine vodka and Grand Marnier in mixing glass. Stir and strain into martini glass. Layer with absinthe. Garnish with orange zest. Stir in orange juice as you serve.

PERSEPHONE
Large martini glass

[137]

20 ml lime juice
20 ml cinnamon-infused sugar syrup
20 ml pomegranate liqueur
40 ml white rum

Shake all ingredients and strain into large martini glass.

Rockabilly

LET'S HAVE A PARTY

The Collins Kids dewy-eyed single, Beetle Bug Bop, and Wanda Jackson's 1960 hit, *Let's Have A Party*, are Rockabilly classics. This was an era that was all about observing the status quo with a smile; when songs were held together by a timeless formula that included simple guitar licks, rhyming vocals, stand-up bass slaps and a heavy snare drum backbeat to boot.

In the 1950's love was apparently easier to find than it is in these jaded times. Back then gentlemen had manners and courting was taken seriously. Girls never refused an offer to dance and it was the in-thing to do on a Saturday night.

It was a time when dancehalls were packed with rockers losing themselves in the jive. Some opted for the Mashed Potato while others liked to Bop. Hot-rods, fancy hair-dos and Sun Records were all part of the décor in the 1950s.

The 'Louisiana Hayride' – a radio broadcast that began in 1948 and became a TV show in the '50s – was where Elvis Presley shook his blue suede shoes. But it was the TV hit show, 'Ranch Party', that saw everyone from Wanda Jackson, the Queen of Rockabilly herself, to The Collins Kids nailing that Hillbilly–Rockabilly crossover live-to-air.

The revival of rockabilly in modern music comes from a place of longing and a desire to bring good old-fashioned innocence back to town. With its catchy, danceable beats Rockabilly takes us back to an era when Rock 'n' Roll, Blues and Hillbilly lived in harmony, holding hands on a porch chasing the all-American dream.

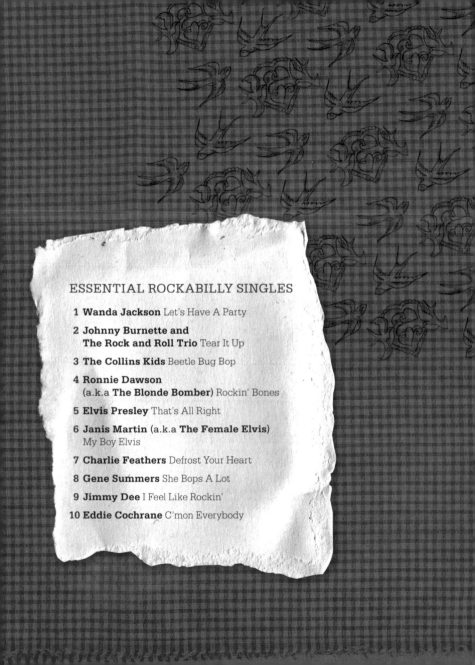

ESSENTIAL ROCKABILLY SINGLES

1 **Wanda Jackson** Let's Have A Party

2 **Johnny Burnette and The Rock and Roll Trio** Tear It Up

3 **The Collins Kids** Beetle Bug Bop

4 **Ronnie Dawson (a.k.a The Blonde Bomber)** Rockin' Bones

5 **Elvis Presley** That's All Right

6 **Janis Martin (a.k.a The Female Elvis)** My Boy Elvis

7 **Charlie Feathers** Defrost Your Heart

8 **Gene Summers** She Bops A Lot

9 **Jimmy Dee** I Feel Like Rockin'

10 **Eddie Cochrane** C'mon Everybody

HIBISCUS HONEYMOON
Collins glass

60 ml tequila
30 ml lemon juice
15 ml honey
60 ml hibiscus juice
a basil leaf to garnish

Shake all ingredients except for garnish and strain into a collins glass over ice cubes. Float the basil leaf to garnish.

BURNT ORANGE BOURBON SOUR
Large old-fashioned glass

3 slices of orange
2 teaspoons castor sugar
splash of rum
60 ml Tennessee whiskey
30 ml lemon juice
15 ml caramel sugar syrup
15 ml orange juice
dash of bitters

Arrange orange slices on plate and sprinkle with castor sugar. Pour on rum and ignite. Combine remaining ingredients in shaker and add 2 of the burning orange slices (reserve the 3rd slice to garnish). Shake and strain into a double old-fashioned glass over ice cubes. Garnish with remaining orange slice.

MEANY-GREENY-BEANY-MARTINI
Martini glass

6 fresh green beans
30 ml gin
15 ml apricot brandy
10 ml jasmine syrup
20 ml lime juice
30 ml apple juice
2–3 extra green beans to garnish

Muddle green beans in shaker. Add all remaining ingredients except for garnish. Shake and double-strain into stemmed martini glass. Garnish with skewered green beans.

CHEESECAKE RODRIGUEZ
Champagne flute

45 ml Licor 43
15 ml lemon juice
15 ml lime juice
10 ml orange syrup
dash of orange bitters
dash of egg white
splash of prosecco
twist of orange and ½ split vanilla bean
    to garnish

Combine all ingredients, except for prosecco and garnish. Shake and double-strain into Champagne flute. Top up with prosecco and garnish with twist of orange and vanilla bean.

PILLOW TALK
Champagne flute

2 strawberries
5 ml apple juice
15 ml strawberry liqueur
15 ml apple liqueur
10 ml bourbon vanilla
splash of Champagne
extra strawberry to garnish

Muddle strawberries in shaker. Add all remaining ingredients except for Champagne and garnish and shake with ice. Double-strain into flute. Top up with Champagne and garnish with a strawberry.

PRINCESS
Champagne flute

1 lime wedge
caster sugar
1 tablespoon mixed berries
40 ml mango liqueur
30 ml guava juice
splash of sparkling rosé

Neatly rub rim of champagne flute with lime juice and dip in sugar.

Place the berries in the bottom of the flute. Combine the mango liqueur and guava juice in a shaker, then shake and double-strain over berries. Top with sparkling rosé.

ROCKY ROAD

Martini glass

5 ml Frangelico
30 ml marshmallow-infused vodka*
10 ml cherry brandy
10 ml dark crème de cacao
10 ml black raspberry liqueur
15 ml soy milk
vodka-soaked marshmallow, grated
    chocolate and chopped hazelnuts
    to garnish

Rim glass with Frangelico.

Combine all remaining ingredients except
for garnish in a mixing glass and stir well.
Pour into martini glass and garnish with
marshmallow, chocolate and hazelnuts.

* *To infuse vodka with marshmallows, combine a 250 g pack of vanilla*
  marshmallows with 700 ml vodka in a microwave-safe bowl. Microwave
  on high for 1 minute. Stir thoroughly then microwave on high for another
  minutes. Leave to stand for 5 minutes. Pour into a bottle ready for use.

PATTY'S POISON

[145]

Beer mug

60 ml passionfruit and cognac liqueur
15 ml golden rum
15 ml banana liqueur
50 ml pineapple juice
splash of soda water
slice of orange and maraschino cherry
**   to garnish**

Combine all ingredients except for soda
and garnish. Shake and pour into beer
mug over ice. Top up with soda and
garnish with orange and cherry.

CINNAMON APPLE

Martini glass

1 small apple, diced
30 ml amaretto
30 ml apple liqueur
60 ml apple juice

Muddle apple and amaretto in shaker.
Add remaining ingredients and shake
with 2 heaped tablespoons crushed ice.
Pour into martini glass with cinnamon-
sugar-crusted rim.

PLANTERS PUNCH

Highball glass

45 ml tequila
20 ml Cointreau
15 ml lemon juice
15 ml pineapple juice
15 ml orange juice
dash of grenadine
slice of orange and maraschino cherry
**   to garnish**

Combine all ingredients except for
garnish and shake with ice. Strain into
highball glass and garnish with orange
slice and cherry.

LAGERITA
Boston glass

30 ml tequila
30 ml lime juice
10 ml agave syrup
splash of wheat beer

Shake tequila, lime juice and syrup.
Strain over ice into glass with salt-crusted
rim. Top up with beer.

BLUE RINSE
Martini glass

75 ml raspberry vodka
30 ml sour mix
1 tablespoon black raspberry liqueur

Shake vodka and sour mix and strain
into martini glass. Float black raspberry
liqueur to create layered effect

PRETTY IN PINK
Beer mug

15 ml vodka
60 ml passionfruit liqueur
45 ml pineapple juice
maraschino cherry to garnish

Shake all ingredients except for garnish
and strain into mug over ice. Garnish
with cherry.

THE ROCKABILLY BARFLY
Pint glass

½ lime
120 ml tomato juice
dash of Worcestershire sauce
dash of Tabasco
1 small bottle Mexican beer
    (Corona or Tecate)
lemon wedge to garnish

Squeeze lime into shaker with 4 ice
cubes. Add tomato juice, Worcerstershire
sauce and Tabasco and shake. Pour
into glass with salt-crusted rim. Top up
carefully with two parts beer and garnish
with lemon wedge.

'ROUND MIDNIGHT
Highball glass

1 teaspoon honey
¼ fresh pear, roughly chopped
6–8 mint leaves
30 ml pear nectar
juice of ½ lime
30 ml pear vodka
15 ml walnut liqueur
15 ml honey-infused vodka

Lightly brush the inside of the highball
glass with honey.

Muddle pear, mint leaves, nectar and
lime juice in shaker. Add remaining
ingredients and shake with ice. Strain
into highball glass over ice cubes.
Top with shaved ice.

SMOKED ALMOND MARTINI
Martini glass

45 ml whisky
15 ml amaretto
5 ml fino sherry
5 ml bourbon vanilla
smoked almonds to garnish

Stir all ingredients except for garnish
in mixing glass then strain into martini
glass. Serve martini glass on a plate and
garnish with smoked almonds.

JOHNNY B GOOD AT IT
Sling glass

45 ml vodka
15 ml green apple liqueur
60 ml white peach purée
30 ml sweet and sour mix
45 ml apple juice

Shake all ingredients with ice
in a rock 'n' roll manner and
dump unceremoniously into
sling glass.

TAKE ME HOME TONIGHT
Sling glass

45 ml vodka
15 ml mandarin liqueur
30 ml lemon juice
15–30 ml sugar syrup
90 ml soda water

Combine all ingredients in an ice-filled shaker. Shake like the blazes and dump into sling glass. Top up with soda water.

GINGER HONEYSUCKLE
Martini glass

60 ml premium rum
30 ml lime juice
20 ml honey water
10 ml ginger juice

Shake ingredients and double-strain into martini glass.

SAGE AND THE GIANT PEACH

Martini glass

½ white peach, roughly chopped
6 sage leaves
60 ml tequila
2 drops of peach bitters
20 ml lime juice
5 ml agave nectar
peach slices to garnish

Muddle peach and sage leaves in shaker.
Add all remaining ingredients except
for garnish and shake. Double-strain
into martini glass and garnish with
peach slices.

GRINGO SLING

Sling glass

45 ml tequila
15 ml Drambuie
10 ml elderflower syrup
20 ml apple juice
15 ml lemon
dash of pomegranate syrup
splash of Champagne or sparkling wine
5 mint leaves

Shake all ingredients except for
Champagne and garnish and pour into
sling glass. Top up with Champagne
or sparkling wine and garnish with
mint leaves.

SINGLE BLOSSOM
Old-fashioned glass

3 slices of grilled lemon
1 teaspoon marmalade
45 ml vodka
25 ml rosemary syrup
3 dashes of lemon bitters
twist of orange to garnish

Place lemon slices in old-fashioned glass
and add marmalade and a third of the
vodka. Stir until marmalade dissolves.
Add rosemary syrup, bitters and another
third of vodka with 6 ice cubes. Stir well
then add remaining vodka. Fill to top with
ice and garnish with orange twist.

HELLO KITTY
Martini glass

30 ml sauvignon blanc
30 ml guava juice
30 ml pink grapefruit juice
15 ml lemon juice
10 ml peach liqueur
5 ml vanilla-infused sugar syrup
pink poki stick to garnish

Shake all ingredients except for garnish
then double-strain into martini glass.
Garnish with a pink poki stick

WANDA JACKSON
Champagne glass

2 teaspoons rhubarb preserves
30 ml gin
15 ml crème de mûres
15 ml lime juice
splash of prosecco

Shake all ingredients except for prosecco and double-strain into flute. Top-up with prosecco.

FOOL'S GOLD
Wine glass

50 ml tequila
10 ml apricot liqueur
10 ml lemon juice
2 teaspoons apricot jam
2 drops of rosewater
dash of bitters
twist of lemon peel to garnish

Shake all ingredients and double-strain into wine glass. Garnish with twist of lemon peel.

COUNTRY

RING OF FIRE

Country music is the refuge of the broken-hearted and those in search of redemption. Some folk like to nurse an emotional hangover with a Country twang, while others analyse life's purpose and their place in it through Country's sad repertoire. Sorrowful obsessions, spiritual enlightenment and inner dialogue with a supreme being are some of Country's characteristics.

One of the genre's leading exponents, Johnny Cash, was a man who evolved from drifting outlaw to reformed evangelist seeking God's salvation. He was a man who walked the line and took the necessary steps to ignore the division in the road ahead. Yet Cash's personal experiences gave his music its glow. And it is this kind of poker-faced realism that gives Country music its edge.

The late Townes Van Zandt once said that his own songs weren't sad, they were hopeless. This country/folk poet spoke about Country's ability to pull you through the dark and windy journey of self-analysis, while always providing the comfort of a roof over your head.

Hank Williams, a twentieth century pioneer of Country music, sang heartbroken songs like *Lovesick Blues* and *Cold Cold Heart*, offering affirmation and reassurance to those who wear their hearts on their sleeves. Country has always stood the test of time, its weathered dialogue providing shelter to drifters and seekers alike.

TOP 10 COUNTRY RECORDS

1 **Waylon Jennings** Honky Tonk Heroes

2 **Willie Nelson** Shotgun Willie

3 **Johnny Cash** At Folsom Prison

4 **Dwight Yoakam** Hillbilly Deluxe

5 **Hank Williams** The Original Singles Collection

6 **Steve Earle** Guitar Town

7 **Emmylou Harris** Evangeline

8 **Lucinda Williams** Car Wheels On A Gravel Road

9 **Billy Joe Shaver** Restless Wind

10 **Merle Haggard** Down Every Road (1962-1994)

HIGHLAND ROSE
Martini glass

2 teaspoons fresh pomegranate seeds
5 mint leaves
45 ml rose- and cucumber-infused gin
15 ml rose liqueur
20 ml lemon juice
½ egg white
2 rose leaves and 1 mint leaf to garnish

Muddle the pomegranate seeds to release the juice. Clap the mint to release flavour (don't muddle it) and add with all the remaining ingredients except for garnish. Shake with ice until the egg white foams. Double-strain into martini glass. Garnish with rose leaves on the rim and float the mint leaf.

RING OF FIRE
Coupette glass

45 ml chilli-infused tequila
30 ml limoncello
5 ml pomegranate molasses

Blend ingredients with ice. Serve in salt–encrusted coupette glass.

GRAVEYARD TRAIN
Sling glass

10 ml Tennessee whiskey
10 ml rum
10 ml Canadian whisky
10 ml tequila
10 ml Grand Marnier
10 ml Drambuie
20 ml lemon juice
splash of cola
lemon wedge and marachino cherry
to garnish

Shake all ingredients except for cola
and garnish then strain over ice cubes.
Top up with cola and garnish with
lemon wedge and cherry.

PRINCESS BRIDE
Martini glass

30 ml white rum
30 ml vanilla liqueur
15 ml lemon juice
15 ml cloudy apple juice
15 ml passionfruit pulp
½ egg white
apple slices to garnish

Combine all ingredients except for
garnish and shake vigorously with
ice. Double-strain into martini glass.
Garnish with apple slices.

VANILLA LAVENDER FIZZ
Highball glass

40 ml gin
10 ml Licor 43
30 ml lemon juice
10 ml vanilla-infused sugar syrup
splash of soda water
sprig of fresh lavender and lemon
**   wedge to garnish**

Shake all ingredients except for soda and
garnish and double-strain into highball
over ice. Top with soda to taste. Garnish
with lavender sprig and lemon wedge.

CARIBBEAN MONK
Old-fashioned glass

2 cm piece banana
40 ml golden rum
10 ml caramel syrup
10 ml Frangelico
20 ml lime juice
dash of egg white
cinnamon powder and pinapple
**   spear to garnish**

Muddle banana. Add all remaining
ingredients except for garnish then shake
and double-strain into glass. Dust with
cinnamon powder and garnish with
pineapple spear.

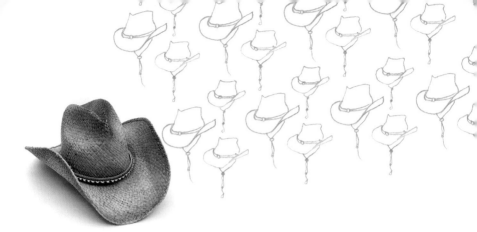

COUP D'ETAT
Martini glass

50 ml vintage rum
10 ml Grand Marnier Cuvée
**   Speciale Cent Cinquantenaire**
30 ml Persian lime juice

Shake ingredients gently and strain
into martini glass.

SANDSTORM
Pilsner glass

15 ml clove-infused white rum
45 ml rum
30 ml lime juice
15 ml maple syrup
30 ml apple juice
30 ml cranberry juice
dash of bitters
pineapple spear and maraschino cherry
**   to garnish**

Shake all ingredients except for garnish.
Strain into a pilsner glass over ice cubes.

Spear pineapple and cherry onto skewer
and use to garnish.

KICKIN KOALA
Old-fashioned glass

30 ml Drambuie
30 ml vodka
15 ml honey liqueur
30 ml lemon juice
15 ml eucalyptus syrup
cracked pepper
dash of bitters
dash of egg white
piece honeycomb to garnish

Shake all ingredients except for garnish and strain into an old-fashioned glass over ice cubes. Float a piece of honeycomb to garnish.

APRICOMB
Martini glass

45 ml honey vodka
15 ml apricot brandy
splash of lime juice
45 ml cranberry juice
1 teaspoon apricot jam
3 dried apricots to garnish

Combine all ingredients except for garnish in shaker then stir in the jam. Shake and double-strain into a chilled martini glass. Spear apricots onto skewer and use to garnish.

HEMINGWAY DAIQUIRI
Martini glass

30 ml rum
15 ml maraschino cherry liqueur
30 ml pink grapefruit juice
15 ml lime juice
10 ml sugar syrup

Shake all ingredients and double-strain into martini glass.

VINTAGE WHITE LADY
Martini glass

45 ml gin
2 teaspoons lemon curd
15 ml Cointreau
dash of egg white

Shake all ingredients and double-strain
into martini glass.

VINYL AGE
Martini glass

½ mandarin (skin on)
sprig rosemary, roughly chopped
30 ml gin
20 ml Pimm's No. 1 Cup
10 ml Campari

Muddle mandarin and rosemary. Shake with remaining ingredients and double-strain into martini glass.

LOKANTA SPECIAL
Highball glass

[167]

¼ lime
45 ml gold rum
5 ml cardamom-infused gomme syrup
5 ml Licor 43
splash of cloudy apple juice

Muddle lime. Add rum and gomme. Stir with crushed ice and float Licor 43 on top. Finish with a splash of apple juice.

SAGE AND BUTTERSCOTCH MARGARITA
Martini glass

½ lime
10 fresh sage leaves, shredded
80 ml butterscotch-infused tequila
10 ml butterscotch schnapps
deep-fried sage leaves and sherbet
   to garnish

Muddle lime with shredded sage and top
with tequila and schnapps. Sit for one
minute to infuse. Shake vigorously and
double-strain into sugar-rimmed martini
glass. Drain deep-fried sage leaves well
and dip in sherbet before using to garnish.

A PASSIONATE AFFAIR
Martini glass

30 ml passionfruit-infused vodka
20 ml vanilla-infused vodka
1–1 ½ teaspoons lychee liqueur
45 ml guava juice
pulp of 1 fresh passionfruit (or four
   teaspoons canned passionfruit pulp
squeeze of lemon
1 mint leaf to garnish

Combine all ingredients except for
garnish and shake with ice. Double-strain
into a chilled martini glass. Float mint leaf
on top.

HAZELNUT CAPRIOSKA

Highball glass

6 lime wedges
1 heaped teaspoon brown sugar
30 ml vodka
30 ml Frangelico
45 ml cranberry juice
slices of lime to garnish

Muddle lime and sugar. Add all remaining ingredients except for garnish and shake well with ice. Pour into a highball glass and top with more crushed ice. Garnish with lime slices.

MAMMA'S MILK
Martini glass

3 strawberries
45 ml vodka
30 ml red wine (preferably
    a good quality shiraz or
    cabernet sauvignon)
20 ml Licor 43
10 ml violet syrup
extra strawberry to garnish

Muddle strawberries well then add
all other ingredients except for
garnish and shake with ice. Double-
strain into chilled martini glass.
Garnish with strawberry.

EASY LIKE SUNDAY MORNING

Sling glass

**30 ml plum Pisco
   (South American brandy)**
15 ml cherry liqueur
15 ml watermelon liqueur
1 tablespoon blueberries
25 ml cranberry juice
30 ml ruby red grapefruit
extra blueberries on skewer to garnish

Combine all ingredients except for garnish, and shake like a good Sunday morning shag. Dump into sling glass and garnish with blueberry skewer.

ONE LAZY AFTERNOON
Martini glass

Grand Marnier to rinse
10 ml Pimms No. 1 Cup
10 ml gin
10 ml lemon juice
15 ml mint- and cucumber-infused
**   gomme syrup**
cucumber twist and caramelised
**   orange zest to garnish**

Rinse martini glass with Grand Marnier.
Combine all ingredients except for
garnish and shake hard with ice. Double-
strain and pour into martini glass. Garnish
with cucumber twist, and float orange
zest on top.

COMME COLLINS
Highball glass

1 lemon, roughly chopped
60 ml gin
30 ml kaffir lime-and lemongrass-
    infused gomme syrup
30 ml soda water
orange twist and maraschino cherry
    to garnish

Muddle lemon with gin and a splash
of gomme syrup. Strain into highball
over ice then top with soda and rest of
gomme. Garnish with orange twist and
maraschino cherry.

PRELL
Highball glass

60 ml vodka
30 ml Midori
60 ml pineapple juice
maraschino cherry to garnish

Shake all ingredients except for garnish
and strain into highball glass. Garnish
with cherry.

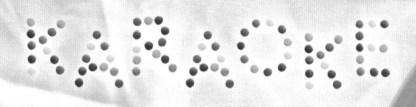

HIT ME WITH YOUR BEST SHOT

Karaoke nights are spontaneous pockets of silliness where you play at being the star and your nearest and dearest are merely victims of your 1980s flashback.

Chicago's *If You Leave Me Now* with all its fevered innuendoes of youth, love and abandonment, is one of those karaoke moments many of us have had, and would rather forget. The sounds of the song's opening chords can immediately wind us back to a time when we found ourselves on stage serenading a lover or a friend possibly even shedding an embarrassed tear or two along the way.

The glory, fight and rivalry of Survivor's *Eye of the Tiger* are delivered best when we punch out the lyrics with passion, while the Righteous Brothers *You've Lost That Lovin' Feelin'* is a cheesy heart-warmer for those who are into sloppy love songs. *Stop Draggin' My Heart Around* by Tom Petty and Stevie Nicks, or Dolly Parton and Kenny Rogers singing *Islands in the Stream* are popular choices for couples and drunken best friends and heck, they're even worth singing with a stranger.

Karaoke nights are about letting loose and channelling the inner wild-child. And so that everyone can enjoy your uninhibited ways, they're enjoyed most when everyone's had a few drinks.

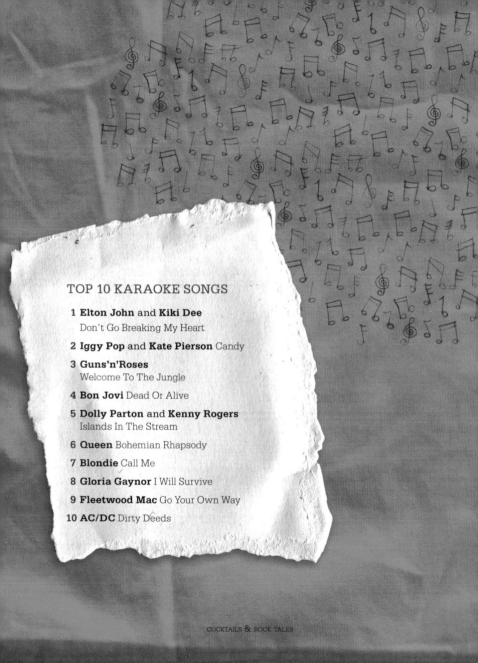

TOP 10 KARAOKE SONGS

1 Elton John and **Kiki Dee**
Don't Go Breaking My Heart

2 Iggy Pop and **Kate Pierson** Candy

3 Guns'n'Roses
Welcome To The Jungle

4 Bon Jovi Dead Or Alive

5 Dolly Parton and **Kenny Rogers**
Islands In The Stream

6 Queen Bohemian Rhapsody

7 Blondie Call Me

8 Gloria Gaynor I Will Survive

9 Fleetwood Mac Go Your Own Way

10 AC/DC Dirty Deeds

MIDNIGHT SPACE RAMBLER

Sling glass

45 ml Tennessee whiskey
15 ml Tuaca
30 ml apple juice
15 ml lemon juice
splash of soda water

Build over ice in sling glass, and top
up with soda water.

CRIMSON AND CLOVER

Martini glass

45 ml vodka
15 ml black raspberry liqueur
15 ml cream
5 ml rosewater
2 teaspoons strawberry jam

Shake all ingredients and double-strain
into martini glass.

PEAR SHAPED
Old-fashioned glass

½ fresh kiwifruit
30 ml kiwi-infused vodka
15 ml Aivy Vodka
15 ml pear liqueur
15 ml lemon juice
20 ml apple juice
5 ml pear concentrate

Muddle kiwifruit. Add all other ingredients and shake with ice. Strain into an old-fashioned glass over ice.

TENTH COLLINS
Highball glass

50 ml gin
20 ml pink grapefruit juice
10 ml lemon juice
15 ml chamomile-infused sugar syrup
30 ml soda water
pink grapefruit wedges and chamomile
    flowers to garnish

Stir all ingredients, except for soda water and garnishes, over ice in a highball glass. Top with soda water and garnish with grapefruit wedges and chamomile flowers.

TEQUILA ESPRESSO MARTINI

Martini glass

60 ml tequila
30 ml espresso coffee
10 ml Kahlúa Especial
10 ml agave nectar

Shake all ingredients and double-strain into a martini glass.

WILD PASSION

Martini glass

45 ml vodka
15 ml Amaro Montenegro liqueur
20 ml lime juice
20 ml passionfruit pulp
15 ml sugar syrup
2 dashes of orange bitters
3 basil leaves

Shake all ingredients and double-strain into a chilled martini glass. Garnish with floating basil leaves.

TURNING JAPANESE
Sling glass

1 lime, quartered
¼ teaspoon green tea powder
10 ml sugar syrup
30 ml white rum
15 ml Midori
30 ml lychee juice
15 ml pineapple juice

Place a lime quarter in a shaker. Add the remaining ingredients and shake well. Pour into sling glass and garnish with 2 more of the lime wedges.

XANADU
Martini glass

15 ml myrtilles (blueberry) purée
30 ml apple juice
squeeze of lime
30 ml vodka
10 ml lychee liqueur
15 ml white crème de cacao
1 fresh lychee soaked in absinthe
to garnish

Combine all ingredients except for garnish. Shake and double-strain into martini glass.

Spear absinthe-soaked lychee on a skewer and ignite. Let burn for 3 seconds then place in drink while still lit.

KARAOKE HIT ME WITH YOUR BEST SHOT

COLD CHISEL SWIZZLE
Highball glass

50 ml bourbon
10 ml fresh ginger juice
10 ml honey water
10 ml lemon juice
dash of bitters
splash of root beer or sarsaparilla
orange slice to garnish

Combine all ingredients except for orange slice in highball glass. Fill three-quarters full with crushed ice and 'swizzle' with a long spoon until glass is frosted. Top with more crushed ice and garnish with orange slice.

TOKYO MARY
Sling glass

30 ml sake
30 ml vodka
60 ml tomato juice
20 ml lemon juice
3 dashes of Tabasco
3 dashes of tamari (Japanese soy sauce)
1 pinch celery salt
1 pinch sea salt
½ teaspoon wasabi paste
½ teaspoon horseradish cream
cracked pepper
cucumber stick to garnish

Combine all ingredients except for garnish and shake well with ice. Strain into sling glass over ice. Garnish with cucumber stick.

THE NUT BAG MARTINI

Martini glass

amaretto to wash
60 ml vodka
20 ml walnut liqueur
10 ml Frangelico
walnut half to garnish

Wash ice cubes with amaretto in a mixing
glass then pour off the amaretto. Stir
remaining ingredients in with ice then
strain into martini glass. Garnish with
walnut half.

JEFFERSON AIRPLANE
Martini glass

50 ml cherry-infused kirsch*
30 ml chestnut liqueur
45 ml port
5 ml Benedictine
tuile wafer to garnish

Shake all ingredients except for garnish
and double-strain into martini glass.
Garnish with tuile wafer.

(kirsch infused with sour cherry jam will do)

BLACKCURRANT CAPRIOSKA
Old-fashioned glass

1 lime, roughly chopped
1 teaspoon vanilla sugar
60 ml currant vodka

Muddle lime with vanilla sugar. Add vodka and stir with crushed ice. Serve in an old-fashioned glass.

FOR THE RECORD
Martini glass

[185]

30 ml citrus-infused vodka
15 ml Cointreau
10 ml black raspberry liqueur
10 ml ginger liqueur
20 ml lime juice
30 ml cranberry juice
dash of orange bitters

Shake all ingredients and double-strain into martini glass.

FRED AND GINGER
Highball glass

3 wedges lemon
⅓ fresh pear
1 cm fresh ginger
8–10 mint leaves
splash of sugar syrup
30 ml white rum
30 ml Tuaca

Muddle lemon wedges, pear ginger,
mint leaves and sugar syrup and
build over crushed ice.

GO FIGURE
Martini glass

45 ml rum
15 ml Licor 43
30 ml fig jam
30 ml lime juice
10 ml vanilla syrup

Shake all ingredients
and double-strain into
martini glass.

APPLESINTHE

Highball glass

30 ml absinthe
30 ml apple liqueur
60 ml apple juice
15 ml lime juice
1 passionfruit, pulp only
apple twirl to garnish

Shake all ingredients with ice. Strain into highball glass. Top with ice and garnish with apple twirl.

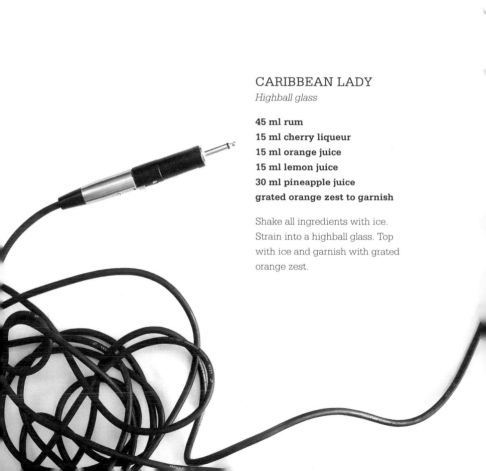

CARIBBEAN LADY
Highball glass

45 ml rum
15 ml cherry liqueur
15 ml orange juice
15 ml lemon juice
30 ml pineapple juice
grated orange zest to garnish

Shake all ingredients with ice.
Strain into a highball glass. Top
with ice and garnish with grated
orange zest.

PLUMSY

[189]

Old-fashioned glass

½ **fresh blood plum**
10 ml vanilla syrup
20 ml passionfruit-infused vodka
20 ml cognac
20 ml lemon juice
15 ml red wine (preferably a decent
    shiraz or cabernet sauvignon)
dash of egg white
2 plum slices to garnish

Muddle the plum and vanilla syrup,
then add all remaining ingredients and
shake with ice. Strain into a old-fashioned
glass over ice cubes and garnish with
plum slices.

SINNERMAN

Large martini glass

½ lemon, roughly chopped
½ orange, roughly chopped
45 ml tequila
15 ml Grand Marnier
5 ml pomegranate molasses

Muddle lemon and orange chunks in
shaker. Add tequila and Grand Marnier
and shake well. Double-strain into a
large martini glass half-rimmed with
cinnamon sugar.

SHELLEY'S SECRET

Martini glass

60 ml gin
30 ml raspberry purée
or blackcurrant juice
3 wedges of lime
twist of lime to garnish

Combine all ingredients except for garnish and shake with ice. Strain into a martini glass and garnish with twist of lime.

HONEY GINGER ZINGER

Collins glass

45 ml honey-infused vokda
10 ml lime juice
10 ml ginger juice
15 ml ginger liqueur
5 ml honey water
lime wedge to garnish

Build all ingredients except for garnish in collins glass. Garnish with lime wedge.

SANGRÍA DE VINO TINTO
Martini glass

30 ml brandy
30 ml shiraz
30 ml blood orange juice
15 ml Grand Marnier
3 lime wedges
slice of orange and slice or lemon
to garnish

Shake all ingredients except for garnish
with ice. Strain into a martini glass and
garnish with slices of orange and lemon.

PHIL COLLINS
Highball glass

10 fresh raspberries
1 teaspoon sugar
juice of 1 large lemon
45 ml gin
15 ml crème de mûres
splash of soda
lemon wedge to garnish

Muddle raspberries, sugar and lemon
juice in highball glass. Fill three-quarters
with ice then add gin and liqueur and
stir. Top with soda and garnish with
lemon wedge.

JOAN COLLINS

Highball glass

6–8 mint leaves
1 teaspoon sugar
juice of 1 large lemon
30 ml gin
30 ml peach liqueur
splash of soda
lemon wedge and mint sprig to garnish

Muddle mint, sugar and lemon juice with
the back of a spoon in highball glass.
Fill three-quarters with ice then add gin
and liqueur and stir. Top with soda and
garnish with lemon wedge and mint sprig.

ACKNOWLEDGEMENTS

This book would not have been possible without the help of
the following bars and bartenders. These drinks belong to them:
Barney Allens at *Possam*, for his amazing contribution and
thanks also to Barney himself; Robb Sloan, Tim Philips and
Cristiano Beretta at *Black Pearl*; Andrew Leonedas at *Blue
Diamond*, Adam Petrie at *Comme*; Sunny Lauren King and
Cal Reynolds at *Ding Dong Lounge*; Marcus Motteram at *Ffour*;
Alex Ross at *Ginger*, for helping me with both this book and
my first one, as well her team of makers and shakers: Gerard
McAlpine, Matt Preisinger, Nathan Taylor and James Roberts;
Misty Hoeta at *Golden Monkey*; Jennifer 'Blackbird' Kippenberger
at *Horse Bazaar*; Brett Smith at *Kelvin*; Josh Davidson at
Lily Blacks; Benjamin Luzz at *Madame Brussels*; Michael Caille
at *Mother's Milk*; Jodi Ham *at* Motor City Bar; Greg Sanderson
at *Murmur*; cocktail creators Luke Harvey, Adam Johanessen,
Darren Eaton and the gorgeous Kellie May Grigons at *The Order
of Melbourne*; Enzo and Mary Pollifroni, Mandy Knight,
Justin Ashworth and bar manager Dave Whitehead at
Polly; Leigh Oliver at *Recorded Music Salon*; Jason Cheung
at *Seamstress*; Maslyn Salt at *Section 8*; Jason Williams at
Sweatshop; Graham Northwood at *The Beauty Bar*; Adam Paurini
at *The Croft Institute*; Alesandra De Luca, Warwick Harty, Mikey
Catalano and David Eddy at *The Melbourne Supper Club + Siglo*;
Andy Griffiths at *Toff In Town* and Nell Mellon and Steve Pang at
Otto's Shrunken Head.

Back in Melbourne I'd like to thank my publisher, Hardie Grant,
for encouraging me to write a second book that combines my
love of cocktails with my other great passion – rock music!
I'd especially like to thank Mary Small, Ellie Smith and
Jane Grant, and my editor, Lucy Malouf. I'd also like to thank
Tim James for his brilliant photographs and Trisha Garner and
Michelle Mackintosh for the gorgeous illustrations and designs:
together, they bring both the rock and cocktails to life on the pages!

I'd like to thank my mum and dad for just being there and for supporting my desire to travel and follow my heart at all costs.

Special thanks go to friends who helped with the book by sharing in the tears of joy and the sheer madness of the entire process. They include: Mishell Vreman (thanks for the prop assistance – magic carpet rides changed our life); Johanna Greenway (for her amazing encouragement and props); Daniel Stewart (for his punk tips); Vanessa Bassili (we might be sisters, but you'll never know); Mary Mihelakos (for all her generosity in providing the paraphernalia needed to make this book); Catherine Haridy; Katy Steele (for her warm hugs and support); Marisol and Jens (my NYC driving force); Ron Heathman (for the late night brain storming sessions and for teaching me a new way to breathe – I take a bow for that Psychedelic and Country top 10) and the Supersuckers; April Dion (my Los Angeles saviour); Lisa Camillo; Lisa Thurbon; Dave Seaborn; Clinton Stewart (for Indie and Karaoke suggestions); Alexia Kannas (my soul sister and for all those re-reads); Pierre Baroni (for his contribution to the Soul chapter and top 10 singles); Jane Kitagawa (for Karaoke suggestions); Bill Nolan; McKenna and Adrianna Ault (for their timeless NYC love); Emilio and Rosa D'Ambrosio and Wayne Slattery.

My life would not be complete without my New York City connection. It's my second home of favourite bars and the home of many amazing people who have helped me over the years. Kisses and love go to: *Motor City Bar* (Jodi Ham and Angela Cerrafuti) – bow to the ladies who bend over backwards for rock'n'roll. This bar has been kicking for ten years and still going strong. *Otto's Shrunken Head*, the best bar in the East Village – check it out next time you hit the streets of East 14th between Avenues A and B.

A massive salute to all the bars that fed me the fuel that kick-started these stories. Your drinks are worth every tasty sip – and this book wouldn't exist if it wasn't for their generous contribution.

[195]

INDEX